Cosplay in Libraries

How to Embrace Costume Play in Your Library

Ellyssa Kroski

ROWMAN & LITTLEFIELD
Lanham • Boulder • New York • London

Published by Rowman & Littlefield
A wholly owned subsidiary of The Rowman & Littlefield Publishing Group, Inc.
4501 Forbes Boulevard, Suite 200, Lanham, Maryland 20706
www.rowman.com

Unit A, Whitacre Mews, 26-34 Stannary Street, London SE11 4AB

British Library Cataloguing in Publication Information Available

Library of Congress Cataloging-in-Publication Data
Kroski, Ellyssa.
  Cosplay in libraries : how to embrace costume play in your library / Ellyssa Kroski.
    pages cm
  Includes bibliographical references and index.
  ISBN 978-1-4422-5647-7 (cloth : alk. paper) — ISBN 978-1-4422-5648-4 (pbk. : alk. paper) — ISBN 978-1-4422-5649-1 (ebook) 1. Libraries—Activity programs. 2. Cosplay. I. Title.
  Z716.33.K76 2015
  025.5—dc23
                                                                    2015020122

Printed in the United States of America

To the vibrant and spirited cosplay community

Contents

Foreword

"Aren't you Princess Leia?" a patron asked me at an evening program.

"Yes, and I am also the Library Director."

When you live in the world of fandoms and libraries, this is a typical exchange.

My personal connection is why I am so excited to see *Cosplay in Libraries* by Ellyssa Kroski, an extremely relevant book for the ubiquitous rise of cosplay in our libraries. There is no one more credible to write this book for our profession than this award-winning librarian, who is also a cosplayer! The author gives practical advice with creative projects to bring cosplay alive for your community.

Our patrons are looking for guidance and instruction on cosplay techniques and trends, and librarians have always sought to connect our physical collections to programs. With cosplay and costuming, we are promoting sci-fi, comic books, TV, film, video games, Japanese animation and works of literature. Libraries host anime and manga clubs and run comic-cons. This book is full of ideas, advice, and step-by-step instructions to run your own successful events!

It is a comprehensive source on ideas to incorporate library makerspaces to allow for skill building and creativity by having programs with sewing machines and 3-D printers. Maybe your library can 3-D print a copy of a Princess Leia blaster, like my own, and I point it out to people interested in our costumes and suggest they check out their public library's maker projects. In the "Getting Started: Tools of the Trade" chapter, methods and materials to design costumes and props are listed with tutorials on Worbla to wigs and makeup.

In the "Places to Go" chapter, you can find the major comic and anime cons, and how to find your local cosplay community, so savvy librarians can partner with these groups. In the "Must-Have Cosplay Resources," the best and latest cosplay websites, magazines, books, apps, and social media groups can be used to inform and be a gateway to this world.

A full chapter on libraries embracing cosplay events through cosplay days, lock-ins, Tosho cons and a Harry Potter Yule Ball walks you through how to do these events yourself. An extremely popular event at my library is a Time Lord Bash for Whovians—*Doctor Who* fans—with a cosplay contest spanning the years of the series. This summer, we are having a Princess Bride cosplay event—"As you wish!"

The earliest costuming at my libraries was through the 501st and the Rebel Legion, the official *Star Wars* costuming groups. With exacting standards that must meet movie quality replicas, *Star Wars* character visits are a highlight of the year for many libraries.

Forward-thinking libraries remain relevant by tapping into trends and technologies, and this book is the first to be a practical guide in which librarians can stay relevant and meet patron expectations.

Cosplayers don't limit themselves by race, gender, age, ethnicity, and this fits our public library access for all philosophy. Crossplay, in which you cosplay with a gender switch, provides great opportunities to discuss body image, gender, and sexual identity.

No one can know about every pop culture genre, so this book allows those invaluable resources and insight. You have a treat in store for you with this book, it gives you all the tools, resources, and ideas that can lead successful and popular events!

The Force runs strong in my family,

—Laverne Mann, MLIS
Director, Cherry Hill Public Library
Cherry Hill, New Jersey
Twitter: @redheadfangirl

Preface

Cosplay, comics, anime, and geek culture have exploded into the mainstream over recent years and have resulted in a thriving community of costume enthusiasts and pop culture fans. Today's cosplayers find inspiration on the pages of comics, anime, classic literature, and even history, as well as film, television, and video games, to inform their creative and oftentimes elaborate ensembles. They use all manner of materials and techniques, including 3-D printers, thermoplastics, craft foam, fabric, and more to design their costumes and props. Libraries on the leading edge are already embracing this new worldwide sensation by integrating cosplay into their programming and events. Learn all about the world of cosplay and how you can host cosplay events, workshops, makerspaces, clubs, and more in your library!

This book will introduce readers to the fascinating world of cosplay, which has become an international sensation and has been photographed and discussed across all types of media outlets, featured in mainstream television series, and can be spotted at nearly every pop culture convention today. This guide will take librarians on a tour of all of the major tools, materials, and technologies that these costumers are using in order to bring their creations to life and will introduce them to comic book, anime, and pop culture conventions; major cosplayers; and cosplay groups, as well as the larger cosplay community. Readers will be walked through a host of projects that they can implement in their libraries right now, ranging from how to organize a comic con in their library to how to host cosplay contests, hold armor-building workshops, budget cosplay events, host 3-D printing prop-making workshops, and much more. Compelling case studies examining libraries that have successfully integrated cosplay programming such as library lock-ins, fandom events, and anime cons are also detailed. And finally, issues important in the cosplay community, such as sexual harassment, body image, and safety, are discussed, and an extensive resources list is provided.

One of my first cosplay experiences was in the summer of 2012 when Midtown Comics put out a call for Marvel cosplayers to take part in the filming of TLC's *Cake Boss* TV show for a special episode dedicated to Spider-Man's fiftieth anniversary. I didn't know much about creating my own costumes at that point, but I pieced together a bunch of items that I had in my closet to create an Emma Frost costume and sent in a photo. I loved January Jones's portrayal of the character in the *X-Men: First Class* movie, and I had wanted to cosplay her version ever since seeing the film. When I got the e-mail that I was chosen, I was pretty nervous; I didn't know anyone who was going, and I had never been to an event like this, so I had no idea what to expect. The filming took place on a rooftop in Chelsea with a breathtaking view of Manhattan. I walked into the shoot feeling completely out of my element and left it having had the time of my life. It was one of the most upbeat and social events I had ever been to. It was like being an instant part of a new community or a secret club. No one criticized my thrown-together costume or my wig (which wasn't great), and no one was standoffish, just the opposite, in fact; everyone was welcoming, friendly, and supportive of one another. Introductions were easy and informal and many consisted of "Hi, can I have a picture with you?" While we waited in between takes, we socialized, took a million photos, exchanged Facebook details, and ate cake . . . lots and lots of cake! See figure 1 for a group shot of the *Cake Boss* cosplayers.

I have experienced that same atmosphere at events of all sizes and types, including massively crowded conventions in other cities. There is a genuine camaraderie and sense of unity among cosplayers, who have a very identifiable way of recognizing others who are kindred spirits—they are all in costume.[1] And it was that feeling of authentic community that first got me hooked on cosplay. Now that I have been cosplaying for a few years, I have added to my reasons for cosplaying the gratifying sense of accomplishment that comes from creating something that I thought was impossible for me to make. In the past few years, I have created my own costumes, props, and weapons, and as someone who had never before used tools such as saws and wire-cutters or even spray paint, I can tell you that it is an incredibly rewarding and empowering feeling of achievement when a costume is completed or a prop is ready to use.

While this is written for librarians of all types who are interested in bringing cosplay into their libraries, it will also appeal to makers and cosplayers themselves, who will benefit from the projects herein. Cosplay programming has potential for many library types, including public, school, and academic libraries.

NOTE

1. Jayme Rebecca Taylor, "Convention Cosplay: Subversive Potential in Anime Fandom" (master's thesis, University of British Columbia, 2009), 18.

Acknowledgments

I would like to heartily thank all of the generous librarians who kindly donated their time to share their expertise and experience to inform both the case studies as well as the projects in this book. I'd also like to acknowledge and thank all of the talented cosplayers and photographers who contributed their work so that I could share it with you. A special thank-you to Chad Mairn and Svetlana Quindt, who both provided essential guidance and contributions to this work.

1

What Is Cosplay?

Cosplay is the activity of dressing up in costume as an admired character in order to express one's enthusiasm and fandom. It is a mash-up of the terms *costume* and *play* and was first coined by writer Nobuyuki Takahashi in the June 1983 issue of *MyAnime* as a way to describe the costumed attendees at the Comiket convention in Tokyo.[1] Cosplay regularly occurs at comic book, pop culture, and anime conventions throughout the world, and dedicated cosplayers will oftentimes travel outside of their local area in order to attend these fan events. Cosplay is a very social activity, and those who participate enjoy an innate sense of community with other costume-goers at these events. Cosplayers take great pride in creating their own costumes for conventions and other happenings, whether by sewing an outfit, crafting a suit of armor, or piecing together an ensemble from clever thrift-store shopping.[2] This fun and exciting pastime involves adopting not only the dress of a particular character but oftentimes their personality traits and idiosyncrasies, distinctive poses for photos, and trademark quotes for interviews and social interactions.[3]

INSPIRATION

Cosplayers find their inspiration from a number of different outlets and genres, including science fiction, comic books, Japanese animation, television, film, video games, and even from works of literature. Most choose a character that they find a particular resonance with or that may represent an aspect of their personality that they want to convey or explore, while others may select a character based on that character's attire.[4] Some cosplayers will attempt to re-create their character's costume as accurately as possible down to the smallest detail, while others will reinterpret their character's clothing or uniform in order to add a new perspective to the ensemble. Cosplayers do not limit themselves to portraying characters within their own race, age group, ethnicity, or even gender. This type of creative expression, which involves dressing up in costume and attending events as an alternate personality, is both an empowering and exhilarating experience for cosplayers, who revel in the ability to transcend societal and cultural limitations through art and play.[5]

HISTORY

Although cosplay has celebrated a recent spike in popularity and general mainstream adoption, it is not a new leisure activity. Cosplay has been chronicled at conventions as early as the first Worldcon (World Science Fiction Convention) in New York City in 1939, at which Forrest J. Ackerman appeared in a futuristic costume in order to help promote the event. *Star Wars* costumers peppered American science fiction and pop culture conventions during the latter part of the 1970s, while Japanese college students masqueraded as anime and manga characters on the other side of the globe. Cosplay continued to gain traction in the 1980s—which, according to Pierre Pettinger, chief archivist of the International Costumers' Guild, was the height of the Worldcon masquerade competitions—and right into the 1990s and 2000s.[6] We now find ourselves in an era of cosplay, most evident at today's conventions, which host exhibit halls teeming with costumed fans.

DEMOGRAPHICS

For forty-six years, the Comic-Con International convention in San Diego, California, has been creating a carnival of comic book, science fiction, film, television, video game, and entertainment-related programming, events, and merchandise.[7] The longest continuously run comic book and popular arts convention in the United States, this pop culture paradise attracts approximately 130,000 eager fans to its four-day event, many of whom are cosplayers.[8] The annual Masquerade costume competition at the con draws a crowd of nearly four thousand into the convention center's ballroom with an overflow audience of viewers topping two thousand in nearby ballrooms.[9] New York Comic Con boasts similar numbers, with their 2014 attendance records exceeding 151,000 guests,[10] thousands of whom witness the con's Eastern Championships of Cosplay in person while millions of spectators around the world watch the competition via live stream.[11] The World Cosplay Summit, held in Nagoya, Aichi, Japan, is an international cosplay gathering incorporating a competition and cosplay parade. The event, which started in 2003, has grown incrementally year after year and now welcomes twenty-eight countries and regions of the world to compete for the championship.[12] Comic cons, anime cons, and cosplay-related events are held in nearly every state in America,[13] as well as worldwide. There's no denying it, cosplay is a hit . . . a big hit with people of all ages.

Age ranges of cosplayers vary greatly, but the hobby is particularly popular among tweens, teens, and young adults, although there are many mature cosplayers, as well as those who are younger than ten who enjoy the pastime. Anime conventions tend to attract a teen to young adult crowd, while comic cons can see many cosplayers over the age of thirty. While most cosplay demographics are anecdotal, there have been some studies regarding the background of these costume enthusiasts.

A study of some 529 cosplayers over 18 years of age was conducted for the thesis "Cosplay Culture: The Development of Interactive and Living Art through Play" by Ashley Lotecki, which found that the majority of cosplayer respondents were female (76 percent), the average age was 23.8, 72 percent identified their race as "white," and the majority—71 percent—had some postsecondary education.[14] Similarly, authors Robin S. Rosenberg and Andrea M. Letamendi reported in "Expressions of Fandom: Findings from a Psychological Survey of Cosplay and Costume Wear" that 65 percent of their 198 participants were women, 68 percent of whom were Caucasian. Participants' ages ranged from 15 to 50 years, and the average number of years cosplaying was 6.77. [15]

When asked why they cosplayed, the majority of participants listed "fun" as their number one reason with "because I like the character" coming in a close second, followed by "a vehicle for creative/artistic expression." Most respondents spent between $100 and $399 per costume.[16] These motivations and average spending figures align with the previously mentioned Lotecki thesis, which found that the average cost spent per costume was $106.71 and that the top three motivations behind participating in cosplay were "to have fun and be social," "to belong to a community with people that share the same passion," and "to transform fantasy into reality."[17]

WHY COSPLAY AND LIBRARIES?

At this point, you may be intrigued, but you may also be asking yourself, What is the connection between this fun and fanciful hobby and libraries? As you will see from the following chapters, cosplay is a pastime that necessitates skill building in areas such as math, science, engineering, technology, and art, making it an exciting new area of programming for libraries. Libraries can engage patrons of all ages by offering much-needed instruction and guidance in the many techniques and trends involved with cosplay, partnering with their communities in the creation process. Additionally, a great many cosplayers glean their inspiration from reading comic books, graphic novels, and manga, an area of collection development that has recently gained traction as forward-thinking librarians have realized that the visual nature of these publications attract children and teens and can be used to promote literacy.

COMICS AND LITERACY

Comic books have entered the classroom as a tool to encourage multiple literacies. Comic books have been shown to foster visual literacy as children learn to make sense of their sequential art. According to Leoné Tiemensma, "To read comics or a graphic novel the critical skills needed for all reading comprehension are needed. This requires many essential literacy skills, including the ability to understand a sequence of events, to interpret characters' nonverbal gestures, to discern the story's plot, and to make inferences."[18] Comic books encourage reading as an enjoyable pastime and help develop a regular reading habit among children. They are also a fantastic resource for both first- and second-language development. "Comics provides authentic language learning opportunities. . . . The dramatically reduced text of comics makes them manageable and language profitable for even beginning level readers."[19] Additionally, many teachers, as well as organizations such as the Comic Book Project (http://www.comic-bookproject.org), use comics in the classroom to teach not just reading skills but writing ones as well. By encouraging students to plan, sketch, and write their own comic books, instructors pass along the skills needed for storytelling through a visual medium such as character and plot development, dialogue construction, and creating supporting artwork.[20]

Comic book, graphic novel, and manga collections in libraries offer resources that will not only appeal to young readers but will offer them literacy skills as well. The library world has warmed to this idea over the past decade as libraries across the globe have started to acquire collections of these visual materials. Levar Burton summed it up perfectly during his talk at the American Library Association (ALA) 2015 Midwinter Meeting when he said, "If your kid is passionate about superheroes, then dammit, buy them comic books."[21] This sentiment can be developed further by the notion that if your library patrons love reading about superheroes, why not start buying comics for your library's collection? And many libraries are doing just that and more. Libraries are hosting their own comic con events, drawing crowds of thousands to their buildings where they spotlight their comic book and graphic novel collections. Library association conferences include panels and talks such as "How to Host a Library Comic Con" at the 2015 New Jersey Library Association Conference, "Using Comics to Promote Literacy" at the ALA 2015 Midwinter Meeting, and the Long Island Libraries and Pop Culture Conference (LIPopCon) is dedicated to little else—it even has a session titled "The Perks of Being a Cosplayer." The Collaborative Summer Library Program (CSLP) has incorporated comics themes into their 2015 summer reading themes, which are "Every Hero Has a Story" for children and early literacy, "Unmask" for teens, and "Escape the Ordinary Elements" for adults. And the organizers of the Association of College and Research Libraries (ACRL) 2015 Conference encouraged librarians to post photos of themselves to social media as Ms. Marvel with their limited-edition conference poster for a chance to win free accommodations at the conference.

COSPLAY AND STEM SKILLS

Cosplay-related events such as armor building workshops, 3-D printing sessions, and associated technology instruction, and so forth, are sure to attract enthusiastic cosplayers and makers. Many of the skills that can be taught during those sessions are considered a valuable part of STEM (science, technology, engineering, and mathematics) learning. For instance, the craft of sewing involves using spatial reasoning and mathematics to take an idea from pattern to garment,[22] while printing out 3-D costume pieces and props involves first designing 3-D models in computer-aided drafting programs using engineering, math, and technology skill sets. Many libraries have realized this and are already incorporating 3-D printing into their programming. Embracing the do-it-yourself (DIY) maker culture, the Sacramento Public Library has recently launched a "library of things" through which they are offering six sewing machines for loan to patrons who may not be able to afford them and are planning a sewing workshop for interested crafters who would like to learn the skill.[23]

As you will see from the projects provided in chapter 6, there are many opportunities for libraries to offer engaging learning experiences as well as promote literacy through embracing cosplay in libraries. But first let us explore the many tools, places, and people involved with the art of costume play and also discuss how libraries are already on board with this captivating activity.

NOTES

1. Brian Ashcraft and Luke Plunkett, *Cosplay World* (Munich: Prestel, 2014).
2. Jayme Rebecca Taylor, "Convention Cosplay: Subversive Potential in Anime Fandom" (master's thesis, University of British Columbia, 2009), 5–23.
3. Rachel Hui Ying Leng, "Gender, Sexuality, and Cosplay: A Case Study of Male-to-Female Crossplay," *The Phoenix Papers: First Edition*, April 2013, 89–110, http://nrs.harvard.edu/urn-3:HUL .InstRepos:13481274.

4. Taylor, "Convention Cosplay," 5–23.

5. Leng, "Gender, Sexuality, and Cosplay," 91.

6. Ashcraft and Plunkett, *Cosplay World*.

7. "Front Page," Comic-Con International: San Diego, accessed January 20, 2015, http://www.comic-con.org/cci.

8. "About," Comic-Con International: San Diego, accessed January 20, 2015, http://www.comic-con.org/about.

9. "Masquerade," Comic-Con International: San Diego, accessed January 20, 2015, http://www.comic-con.org/cci/masquerade.

10. "NYCC Fan FAQs," New York Comic Con, accessed January 20, 2015, http://www.newyorkcomiccon.com/About/NYCC-Fan-FAQs/.

11. "NYCC Eastern Championships of Cosplay," New York Comic Con, accessed January 20, 2015. http://www.newyorkcomiccon.com/Events/NYCC-Eastern-Championships-of-Cosplay/.

12. "World Cosplay Summit," *Wikipedia*, last modified February 26, 2015, http://en.wikipedia.org/wiki/World_Cosplay_Summit.

13. "Worldwide Conventions Map," Upcoming Cons, accessed January 21, 2015, http://www.upcomingcons.com/map.

14. Ashley Lotecki, "Cosplay Culture: The Development of Interactive and Living Art through Play" (master's thesis, Ryerson University, 2012), 36–37.

15. Robin S. Rosenberg and Andrea M. Letamendi, "Expressions of Fandom: Findings from a Psychological Survey of Cosplay and Costume Wear," *Intensities: The Journal of Cult Media* 5 (Spring/Summer 2013), http://intensitiescultmedia.com, 11, 12.

16. Rosenberg and Letamendi, "Expressions of Fandom."

17. Lotecki, "Cosplay Culture."

18. Leoné Tiemensma, "Visual Literacy: To Comics or Not to Comics? Promoting Literacy Using Comics" (paper presented at World Library and Information Congress, 75th IFLA General Conference and Council, Milan, Italy, August 23–27, 2009).

19. Ibid.

20. "Home Page," The Comic Book Project, accessed February 5, 2015, http://www.comicbookproject.org/.

21. Sanhita SinhaRoy, "LeVar Burton Delights: The Actor and *Reading Rainbow* Host Discusses His Important Influences," *American Libraries*, February 2, 2015, http://americanlibrariesmagazine.org/blogs/the-scoop/levar-burton-delights/.

22. "Front Page," iamcompletegirls, accessed February 2, 2015, http://www.iamcomplete.info/#!sewing-is-steamulating-class/co4y.

23. Ellen Garrison, "Borrow a Sewing Machine? Sacramento Public Library to Start Loaning More Than Books," *Sacramento Bee*, February 1, 2015, http://www.sacbee.com/news/local/education/article8920145.html.

2

Getting Started

Tools of the Trade

There are many methods and materials involved in designing a cosplay costume, and they are all subject to the creativity, taste, skill level, and budget of the cosplayer. What makes cosplay such a fun and enjoyable hobby is the wide range of interpretations possible with every character and costume. Some cosplayers will try and re-create a "screen-accurate" costume, while others will put their own spin on an existing character. I have seen rockabilly versions of Harley Quinn, the Joker, Superman, and Wonder Woman, as well as hipster versions of the Disney princesses; zombified X-Men and other superheroes; a steampunk Deadpool; and a Renaissance-era Hulk, Batman, and Robin. See the photospread in the center of this volume for many cosplay examples. There is no definitive "right way" to cosplay or design a costume.

Cosplayers are incredibly resourceful when it comes to making their costumes and will use all kinds of materials and "found" items, from paper towel cardboard to repurposed children's toys to LED lights. And what's great about the community is that most cosplayers are ready with advice and more than willing to share how they created their costumes through tutorials, videos, Pinterest pins, and even step-by-step progress photos of their creation process.[1] While there is a very wide variety of materials that are used, here are some of the most popular tools of the trade.

CLOTHING

Fabrics and Trim

Sewing a costume from scratch is one of the most well-respected methods of creating a cosplay ensemble and a feat that many cosplayers strive to achieve. The majority of well-known or "cosfamous" cosplayers design and sew their own costumes, many of which are quite elaborate. This is a great opportunity for libraries with makerspaces to offer their communities both access to sewing machines as well as training and technique workshops.

Repurposed Clothes

Since many cosplayers either cannot sew or have limited sewing capabilities, they will oftentimes repurpose clothing that they already have or have purchased specifically for a cosplay costume. Many will go thrift-store shopping in order to find costume pieces cheap, especially when looking for vintage items or very expensive ones, such as gowns. Alternatively, cosplayers will purchase a base item and then customize it to their costume specifications.

Commissions

Another way that many cosplayers will fill their costume closets is by commissioning hard-to-create or unique pieces, such as corsets, hats, helmets, and uniforms, from handcrafters on Etsy or from experts such as Anovos (http://www.anovos.com), which specializes in screen-accurate uniforms and gear for fandoms such as *Star Trek*, *Star Wars*, and *Battlestar Galactica*. Similarly, Organic Armor (http://organicarmor.com) creates custom-made and comfortable armor made with latex, foam, and other lightweight materials. They are particularly known for their elaborate crowns and headdresses. These types of commissioned items are usually quite costly, however, and so are usually purchased as a last resort.

ARMOR AND PROPS

It is quite commonplace to see both male and female con-goers in full suits of armor inspired by comics, anime, science fiction or fantasy films, and video games and even carrying matching swords, staffs, and other larger-than-life weaponry. These impressive armor outfits can be meticulously detailed and oftentimes come complete with an awe-inspiring paint job that includes weathering and even blood spatter, making the cosplayer appear as if they've just stepped out of battle. To the onlooker, it is an absolute mystery as to how these elaborate armor ensembles and accompanying props are constructed; however, this practice is something that every cosplayer, regardless of skill level or pocketbook, can undertake. Armor and props can be built using a number of materials that range in price from the very costly (Worbla) to the nominal (cardboard or paper) and are, therefore, an accessible form of cosplay to all. Of course, they can be made with any number of materials, including leather, wood, metal, and so on. However, the following are the most commonplace materials and tools employed by cosplayers today.

Thermoplastics

Thermoplastics are plastic materials that, when heated, become moldable and flexible. Cosplayers heat these materials using blow dryers or heat guns found at home supply stores and then mold them into armor and props of all types. The two most popular products are Worbla and Wonderflex.

Worbla

Worbla is a thermoplastic made from natural fibers and manufactured by a German company called Rhenoflex, which produces it for industrial shoe making.[2] It is used by cosplayers to create items such as armor, props, masks, helmets, and jewelry. Worbla must be special-ordered online from a supplier such as CosplaySupplies.com and comes in various size sheets. It is the most expensive of all the materials discussed in this chapter at approximately $88 for a jumbo-sized 39.25" × 59" sheet. As it is a thermoplastic, Worbla must be heated to 90°C (194°F) to use; however, it will hold its shape exactly when it is cooled.[3] There are many benefits to choosing Worbla, the most significant being its ability to be molded and stretched into full circle curves, unlike any other material discussed in this chapter. Another advantage is that Worbla has an adhesive side that will stick to itself and/or craft foam when layering materials; therefore, glue is not necessary. Additionally, Worbla can be reheated and remanipulated if mistakes are made, and the scraps left over from cutting out armor pattern pieces (see chapter 6, project 5: "How to Host a Create-Your-Own Armor with Worbla Event") can be combined with each other and then molded like putty into armor details, and so on. The downsides to using Worbla are that the nonglue side of the material has a rough surface that must be primed before painting, and the material can start to get bumpy when heated and shaped too much. Also, Worbla is thinner than Wonderflex (discussed next), and, therefore, not as sturdy; however, most people either stick a layer of craft foam behind each piece of Worbla or make a Worbla-foam-Worbla sandwich with each pattern piece. Worbla is recommended for chestplate armor, round items such as crowns, bracers, and almost any other armor or prop item.[4] See figures 2, 20, and 30 in the photospread for examples of armor crafted with Worbla.

Tutorials

- "How to Create Breastplates with Worbla": https://youtu.be/hXme58f4Ibc
- Worbla tutorials on Pinterest: http://tinyurl.com/mbexdoq
- "How to Worbla: An Introduction": https://youtu.be/JmewudSy9Bg
- How to make Katarina's swords from *League of Legends*: https://youtu.be/yuH7zO-PqP0
- How to fix your armor to your body: https://youtu.be/kujts-8rnPo
- "Worbla Tutorial: How to Make a Superhero Mask (Robin)": https://youtu.be/RUb5yx-2SN4w
- "How to Make Boot/Shoe Armor with Worbla": https://youtu.be/LkEqc_wb304

Wonderflex

Wonderflex is a thermoplastic with a woven adhesive backing on one side, making it look similar to thick duct tape. It is used by cosplayers to build all manner of props and armor items, similar to Worbla. Like Worbla, Wonderflex must be special-ordered by the sheet from an online supplier such as TheEngineerGuy.com.[5] It is much more affordable than Worbla, although pricier than all types of foam, at a rate of approximately $45 for a jumbo, 43" × 55" sheet. In order to use it, Wonderflex must be heated to 70–80°C (158–176°F), and it holds its shape exactly when cooled.[6] It is very durable and is the sturdiest of the thermoplastics. Another benefit of using Wonderflex is that it is also an adhesive and will stick to itself or to foam and other materials when heated. Scraps of Wonderflex that are left over can be combined and used like clay to mold details in armor or other items. And Wonderflex has a smooth side that doesn't need to be primed before painting it. The main disadvantage to choosing Wonderflex is that it is only capable of making bell-shaped curves, not fully circular ones. It can also get bumpy if heated and shaped too much.[7] Wonderflex is recommended for making large curved armor pieces, shields, swords, staffs, and so on.[8]

Tutorials

- "Cosplay Tutorial: Wonderflex Armor—Part 1": https://youtu.be/UUjq3alV13s
- "Cosplay Tutorial: Wonderflex Armor—Part 2": https://youtu.be/9TfL_1cj-mM
- "BLitZ Cosplay Tutorial: The Basics of Wonderflex": https://youtu.be/qzugTUjmIJI
- Wonderflex tutorials on Pinterest: http://tinyurl.com/nzzhpjm

EVA Foam

EVA, or ethylene-vinyl acetate,[9] foam is the type of foam that is used to make yoga mats, floor mats, tile mats, and craft foam such as the sheets that you find at craft supply stores like Michaels. This type of foam is also used by cosplayers to create amazing armor builds, weapons, and props.[10] See figure 3 in the photospread for an example of body armor created with EVA foam.

Tiled Floor and Rolled Mats

Foam tiled floor mats can be found in the automotive or flooring sections of stores such as Home Depot and Walmart and are oftentimes found in tile packs of 2" × 2" with four to six interlocking pieces. Rolled foam mats can be found in 2" × 6" rolls as either flooring or as exercise or yoga mats and can also be found in home supply stores. Rolls and tile packs have finishes such as "diamond plate" or "cross pattern," which are sometimes perfect for armor surfaces. These materials are light and very flexible and much cheaper than thermoplastics at $15–$20 per tile pack and an average of $24 per roll.[11] Both of these foam materials can be heated using the same methods as those used to heat and shape thermoplastics, and their thickness and softness make them both visually appealing and comfortable as armor pieces. Each piece must be superglued or adhered to other parts in order to complete the armor, as this material is not naturally adhesive. Foam will not result in the hardness of the thermo-plastics and is more prone to scratching and scuffing; however, with a good paint job, foam will give the appearance of hard metal armor, just as Worbla and Wonderflex achieve, and the added bulk makes foam perfect for suits such as Iron Man or a Storm Trooper. Fully circular curves cannot be achieved with foam; however, with heat and a bit of finessing, it can be shaped into simple curves. EVA foam tiles and mats are recommended for creating armor pieces, weapons, and props of all types.

Tutorials

- "Introduction to EVA Foam Armor Crafting": http://tinyurl.com/mrdmkrb
- "Build Some Sci Fi Armor for CHEAP: DIY": https://youtu.be/vb6CXGortrQ
- "EVA Foam Armor: The Basics": https://youtu.be/d67ETuMiIiI
- "Crafting a Foam Sword Part 1": https://youtu.be/JOFu0MBAxE4
- "How to Make a Foam Helmet, Tutorial Part 1": https://youtu.be/ODSNPYdvJRo
- "Destiny Hand Cannon Foam Prop": https://youtu.be/jx_CfdAYV7c
- "WM Armory Foam Fabrication Tutorial": https://youtu.be/YbQ2gb_QvFs

Craft Foam

Craft foam can be found in most arts and craft stores. It can be purchased in packs or by the individual sheet. It is available in various sizes, with 9" × 12" sheets being average but ranging up to 12" × 18", and in multiple thicknesses, including 2 mm and 6 mm. Craft foam is very inexpensive at an average of $1 per sheet and can be found in value packs for even less. It can be heated with a hot air gun and will hold its shape when cooled, although not as well as a thermoplastic. It is not as sturdy as some other materials; however, it can be made more durable by backing the foam with fabric or layers of glue. Some cosplayers will spray a layer of Plasti Dip rubber coating onto their props made with craft foam in order to make them more resistant to scratching and easier to paint. Craft foam can be shaped into curves by heating it, but it cannot be made into full curves like a circle. Some craft foam is adhesive but most is not, so some sort of bonding agent is usually needed. Craft foam does not have the issue of getting bumpy when heated as some other materials do. It is smooth on both sides and doesn't need to be sanded and primed before painting. It is recommended for flat armor pieces, wings, props, and armor details.[12] See figure 4 in the photospread for an example of an Infinity Gauntlet created with craft foam.

Tutorials

- "Craft Foam Armor Tutorial—Bracers": https://youtu.be/aS4O6cjSVSc
- "Craft Foam Breastplate Tutorial": https://youtu.be/hj-WC35cxgs
- "Craft Foam Tutorial": https://youtu.be/oNvtMxvaZrg
- "Craft Foam Wings": https://youtu.be/Qn0BDcdnDMg
- Foam Zelda shoulder piece: https://youtu.be/LYenLzKvAyM
- "How to Make Craft Foam Armor for Women": http://tinyurl.com/o6ax3ap

Paper

There are many ways that resourceful cosplayers use paper products to build their costumes from cardboard armor suits to paper molded helmets to papier-mâché props.

Pepakura

Pepakura is a papercraft named for the free software program Pepakura Designer (http://www.tamasoft.co.jp/pepakura-en/) that is capable of creating and viewing 3-D pattern pieces that can be printed out on card stock and then assembled. Cosplayers find existing or create new foldable paper patterns in the Pepakura Designer's Gallery, as well as other websites; print them out; and then cut and fold each piece before assembling them with glue. Assembled pieces are often reinforced with Bondo fiberglass resin and/or automotive filler, sanded, and then painted. Pepakura patterns can easily be edited and their scale adjusted in order to create customized sizes for helmets and armor. Paper pieces that are cut out from the pattern are often numbered; however, with the Pepakura Viewer, each piece can be moused over to see which other piece(s) they attach to and where on the 3-D model the pattern piece is from.[13] These patterns are extremely intricate and involve many, sometimes hundreds of pieces that must be meticulously organized and patiently folded and glued together. Although this is one of the cheapest ways to create armor cosplay builds such as Iron Man and *Halo* helmets and even full suits of armor, it is certainly the most time consuming. Because of the detail of these patterns, Pepakura patterns are also used by those using foam to make their pieces. Pepakura is recommended for making helmets, props, and even armor, but only for the most patient. See figures 5 and 6 in the photospread for examples of full armor created with Pepakura.

Tutorials

- Tamasoft Pepakura Gallery: http://tinyurl.com/9cc4k84
- *Skyrim* Pepakura patterns: http://zombiegrimm.deviantart.com/gallery
- Pepakura and paper projects on Pinterest: http://tinyurl.com/jwjh2g5
- *Halo: Reach* Pepakura files from the 405th Infantry Division: http://tinyurl.com/ojzrvtq

- Measuring, scaling, and sizing Pepakura patterns: https://youtu.be/H_YIKeFX9P8
- "The Ultimate 'How to Make a Paper Sword' Tutorial": https://youtu.be/A9twzsSILUk
- Propzone Pepakura files: http://propzone.be/files.html

Cardboard

Innovative cosplayers can create helmets and, yes, even full suits of armor from folded and bent cardboard and masking tape or hot glue. There are plenty of Pepakura patterns and cardboard helmet, armor, and props tutorials available online that can be followed, or cosplayers can create their own. Cardboard is a sturdy material, which makes the resulting armor tough. It's also the least expensive material for creating cosplay costumes because most cosplayers don't actually purchase the cardboard but instead reuse items they already have, such as pizza boxes and shipping boxes. Cardboard is recommended for making helmets, simple armor suits, and props. See figure 3 in the photospread for an example of a cardboard Judge Dredd helmet.

Tutorials

- "How to Make a Cardboard Minecraft Pickaxe": https://youtu.be/CneZcBZXtu8
- "Stormtrooper Helmet DIY Part 1": https://youtu.be/VbSv0TO4eLQ
- How to make cardboard armor: http://tinyurl.com/ou8r7xe
- "Iron Man Mark 4 Helmet": https://www.youtube.com/watch?v=iAtEuh5JVT8
- "Cosplay Tutorial: How to Make a Helmet out of Cardboard and Masking Tape": https://youtu.be/2yLFlbJLjQ0

Papier-Mâché

Papier-mâché techniques are often used in cosplay to create eye and full-face masks, helmets, and a myriad of props such as skulls, horns, monsters, and weapons. It is also sometimes used to strengthen Pepakura projects. I myself have used papier-mâché to create a large "terror dog" to accompany my Gozer cosplay from the film *Ghostbusters*. Since my cosplay was going to be a bit obscure, I wanted to create a prop that would make it instantly recognizable, and having a giant, leashed demonic dog that I dragged beside me on a barrel roller did just that! I took the tutorials and techniques that I found in the book *Papier-Mâché Monsters: Turn Trinkets and Trash into Magnificent Monstrosities* by Dan Reeder[14] and I designed my own monster using papier- and cloth mâché that was a huge hit and one of my favorite creations to date. And it cost me almost nothing to create. I used my old newspapers and an old worn sheet for materials, along with some polymer clay, which I had hanging around, for the teeth. The only costs I incurred were for the acrylic paints and the barrel roller. See figure 7 in the photospread for an example of a papier-mâché monster companion.

Tutorials

- How to make a Maleficent headpiece with horns: https://youtu.be/y1aBKRcLTmE
- How to make a Haku mask from *Naruto*: https://youtu.be/14XIpaKwZnM
- How to make a mask with paper and foil: https://youtu.be/nMrZy1d-lLY
- "How to Make a Spartan Helmet": https://youtu.be/gE5hL3tC8x0
- "How To: Make a Cubone Costume" (*Pokémon*): https://youtu.be/iGJuVF6osmI
- "Paper Mache Mask Making Tips": https://youtu.be/FhhqxCot5f0

THREE-DIMENSIONAL PRINTED COSPLAY

Three-dimensional (3-D) printers can be used to make all manner of costume pieces and added details, props such as *Star Trek* phasers, Sonic Screwdrivers (*Doctor Who*), full helmets and crowns, as well as jewelry. Cosplayers can find a myriad of patterns on websites such as Thingiverse, which supplies over one hundred thousand "things" as files for free download and use on a 3-D printer. Alternatively, costume makers can use a 3-D modeling software such as Tinkercad to design their own props and pieces to be printed. (See chapter 6, project 4: "How to Host a Cosplay Props 3-D Printing Event.") Three-dimensional printed items are made of a hard plastic that is very durable and resilient and quite easy to paint. See figure 8 in the photospread for an example of 3-D printed cosplay accessories.

Tutorials

- "3D Printing & Design Tutorials" from Shapeways: http://www.shapeways.com/tutorials
- Tinkercad tutorials: https://www.tinkercad.com/about/learn
- Thingiverse models/patterns: http://www.thingiverse.com
- "3D Printing Basics: The Free Beginner's Guide": http://tinyurl.com/kzfuocn
- "How to Get Started with 3D Printing (without Spending a Fortune)": http://tinyurl.com/ktmsqwr

PERSONAL PROTECTIVE EQUIPMENT

Many of the materials, glues, paints, and sealants that cosplayers use can be hazardous if proper safety measures are not taken. Libraries offering hands-on cosplay crafting workshops will want to be sure to have safety equipment available for participants, as well as provide education to cosplayers about the necessity of safety equipment during their own home projects. Although I have chosen materials that are not highly toxic or particularly dangerous for the projects in chapter 6, personal protective equipment (PPE) should still be worn to ensure safety. Cosplayers should wear protective gloves when crafting in order to safeguard skin against chemicals such as glues, cements, primers, and paints, as well as from burning from hot thermoplastics or hot glue. Safety respirators that filter and purify air should be worn when working with chemicals that produce harmful fumes, as well as when sanding materials such as Gesso, which produces a large amount of dust that may make breathing difficult. Protective eyewear or goggles should be worn when working with power tools, liquid chemicals, and any other materials that could cause damage to the eyes. Protective clothing such as long sleeves and pants instead of shorts should also be worn when working with many of these materials. And finally, always work in a well-ventilated space.[15] The number-one rule with crafting and cosplay is to be safe!

WIGS

Wigs have come long way in recent years. It used to be that you could tell if someone was wearing a wig from a mile away, but that's just not so anymore. Today's synthetic wigs are beautiful and affordable, and many of them are heat resistant, so they can be styled with curling and straightening irons, washed, dried with a hair dryer (on low!), and fashioned into stunning styles to accompany cosplay outfits. Wig styling is an art that can easily be learned and is practiced by most cosplayers. Cutting and styling wigs is a particularly important skill to acquire for anime cosplayers, as characters in Japanese animation often have distinctive hairdos. There are many online guides and tutorials, and this would be an excellent opportunity for libraries to provide fun and low-tech programming for would-be stylists through workshops or cosplay wig-styling competitions in the library. See the photospread for many examples of cosplay wig styling.

Tutorials

- Cosplay wig tutorials on Pinterest: https://www.pinterest.com/explore/cosplay-wig-tutorial/
- The A to Zs of Cosplay Wigs: https://youtu.be/pZJi4YU3Xjw
- "The Cosplayer's Wig Styling Essentials": http://tinyurl.com/mj483ly
- "Cosplay 101: Taking Care of Your Wigs": https://youtu.be/q9C2blRBL8M

MAKEUP

Anyone who's ever seen the Syfy reality TV series *Face Off* knows the transformative power of special effects makeup to completely alter the appearance of the wearer. The official sponsor of the show is the Germany-based professional makeup brand Kryolan, which has been supplying the film, television, and theater industries with makeup for nearly seventy years. They offer 16,000 makeup products in 750 colors,[16] and many cosplayers make great use of their body paints, liquid latex, artificial blood, and other special effects offerings. Their products can be found online at https://us.kryolan.com. Another professional makeup company is Ben Nye, which has been around for almost fifty years. Their products have been used in over five hundred feature films,[17] and they offer everything from body tints and prosthetic wounds to bald caps and wrinkle stipple. Their products can be purchased through resellers such as Stage Makeup Online (https://www.stagemakeuponline.com), as well as at some costume stores.

There are countless YouTube videos instructing viewers on how to achieve desired effects for nearly every character on film and TV. Focusing on one or two techniques might be a great idea for a library event or workshop. Why not host a "*Face Off* Day at the Library" in which patrons watch the television show or YouTube tutorials and then are challenged to re-create some of the effects after instruction is provided?

Makeup Tutorials

- Ben Nye YouTube tutorials: https://www.youtube.com/user/BenNyeMakeup
- Kryolan YouTube tutorials: https://www.youtube.com/user/KryolanOfficial
- Zombie FX makeup by Silvia Quiros: https://youtu.be/rkqOI17X4Js
- "Creepy Broken Doll Makeup Tutorial": https://youtu.be/Pj0XNDHYTcY
- "*How to Train Your Dragon*: Toothless Makeup Tutorial": https://www.youtube.com/watch?v=IxDIpwy-cDw
- "*Guardians of the Galaxy*: Gamora Makeup Tutorial": https://youtu.be/LxsXuDrq9hg

THE ART OF REPURPOSING

Not every costume needs to start from scratch. Cosplayers oftentimes reuse elements of previous costumes to create new ones. I myself have used the same exact outfit that I wear to cosplay Chewbacca to transform myself into an Ewok by adding an orange hood and a homemade spear. Likewise, I have reused many elements from my postapocalyptic *Fallout: New Vegas* cosplay to create one appropriate for the new *Mad Max: Fury Road* film. Repurposing and reusing costume pieces is a practice that resourceful cosplayers adhere to as it helps spread their crafting dollars and adds more costumes to their closet.

APPS

Tech-savvy cosplayers use apps to help them plan and find inspiration for their costumes. Here are just a few apps that are useful for cosplayers.

Cosplanner (http://cosplanner.catokusanagi.com)

Available for iOS and Android devices, this free app enables you to manage all of your cosplays, including saving reference images, keeping track of costs, logging events, and more.

Guidebook (https://guidebook.com)

Guidebook is an event app for conferences and conventions that provides maps, schedules, and photos for the event. Many comic and anime cons have their schedules and programs listed within this free app.

Comics by comiXology (http://tinyurl.com/pdtqoqv)

Over fifty thousand digital comics and graphic novels are available from publishers such as Marvel, DC, Image, IDW, Disney, and more through this app.

Marvel Unlimited (http://tinyurl.com/kscm2bf)

Kind of like Netflix for comics, the Marvel Unlimited subscription opens up access to Marvel's back catalog of thirteen thousand issues.

DC Comics (http://tinyurl.com/lat5l8g)

This comic book store app provides access to tales from the DC Universe, including more than one thousand new DC Comics titles annually.

Dark Horse Comics (http://tinyurl.com/k3bd28l)

This app provides a gateway to more than three thousand comics such as *Buffy the Vampire Slayer, Conan, Battlestar Galactica,* and more.

VIZ Manga (http://tinyurl.com/kfqakjw)

The best Japanese manga titles are available through this app, including *Death Note*, *One Piece*, *Dragon Ball*, *Bleach*, *Naruto*, and hundreds more.

NOTES

1. Rachel Hui Ying Leng, "Gender, Sexuality, and Cosplay: A Case Study of Male-to-Female Crossplay," *The Phoenix Papers: First Edition*, April 2013, 89–110, http://nrs.harvard.edu/urn-3:HUL.InstRepos:13481274.

2. Booker, "Cosplay 101: Worbla, the Wonder Thermoplastic FAQ—Part 1," *Charisma Plus 2 Magazine*, March 14, 2013, http://cplus2magazine.com/cosplay-101-worbla-the-wonder-thermoplastic-faq-part-1/.

3. "Worbla Thermoplastic—Jumbo Sheet," CosplaySupplies.com, accessed February 25, 2015, http://www.cosplaysupplies.com/store.php?p=WORB1.

4. Eli Ebberts, "Craft Foam VS. Wonderflex VS. Worbla," *Oh My Cosplay: Eli Ebberts' Cosplay Portfolio* (blog), November 3, 2013, http://ohmycosplay.com/2013/11/03/craft-foam-vs-wonderflex-vs-worbla/.

5. Volpin Props, "Creating Costume Armor with Wonderflex," Instructables, accessed February 25, 2015, http://www.instructables.com/id/Creating-Costume-Armor-with-Wonderflex/.

6. "Wonderflex Basics," CosplaySupplies.com, accessed February 25, 2015, https://www.cosplaysupplies.com/tutorials/wonderflex.

7. Ebberts, "Craft Foam VS. Wonderflex VS. Worbla."

8. "Wonderflex FAQ," CosplaySupplies.com, accessed February 25, 2015, https://www.cosplaysupplies.com/tutorials/wonderflexfaq.

9. "Ethylene-Vinyl Acetate," *Wikipedia*, accessed February 25, 2015, http://en.wikipedia.org/wiki/Ethylene-vinyl_acetate.

10. "EVA Foam Crafting—Part 1," Cosplay Nation, accessed February 25, 2015, http://cosplaynation.net/2013/09/18/eva-foam-crafting-part-1/.

11. Towering Props, "Creating a Costume/Cosplay from E.V.A Foam," Instructables, accessed February 25, 2015, http://www.instructables.com/id/Creating-a-CostumeCosplay-from-EVA-Foam/.

12. Ebberts, "Craft Foam VS. Wonderflex VS. Worbla."

13. Cata, "A Beginner's Guide to Pepakura," OHI Cosplay, accessed March 9, 2015, http://ohicosplay.tumblr.com/post/63666176778/a-beginners-guide-to-pepakura.

14. Dan Reeder, *Papier-Mâché Monsters: Turn Trinkets and Trash into Magnificent Monsters* (Layton, UT: Gibbs Smith, 2009).

15. "PPE: Wearing Proper Gear," *Cosplay Tutorial*, accessed April 7, 2015, http://cosplaytutorial.com/guides/ppe.php.

16. "About Kryolan," Kryolan, accessed April 22, 2015, https://us.kryolan.com/aboutus.

17. "Ben Nye," Stage Makeup Online, accessed April 22, 2015, https://www.stagemakeuponline.com/search?brand=Ben+Nye.

3

Places to Go, People to See

There are many different types of events that encourage people to dress up in costume but none more popular and well attended than the convention. Most comic cons are actually multigenre happenings that gather artists, writers, and comic book aficionados along with film, video game, and TV enthusiasts into a giant celebration of pop culture fandom. In her thesis titled "Convention Cosplay: Subversive Potential in Anime Fandom," Jayme Rebecca Taylor likened Comic-Con to Disneyland, describing it as a place "where families go for a particular experience—walking long distances, waiting in lines, looking for opportunities to see celebrities, and hoping to make 'magical' memories."[1]

Likewise anime cons bring together fans of Japanese animation, manga, film, and culture, while other events amass admirers of video games, literature, or genres such as steampunk, horror, or science fiction and fantasy. And there are many variations on these types of events, such as comic book conventions that concentrate solely on comic art or conventions for a particular film or TV show, for example, the Official *Star Trek* Convention in Las Vegas, which attracts between ten to twelve thousand *Star Trek* fans each year.[2] To illustrate further, here are fifteen of the most popular comic book, anime, pop culture, science fiction, and gaming conventions in North America.[3]

THE MAJOR CONVENTIONS

1. New York Comic Con

http://www.newyorkcomiccon.com
Date: October
Location: New York, NY
Number of Attendees: 151,000+
Type of Event: Comic book and pop culture convention
How Many Days: 4
Date of Origin: 2006

In 2014, New York Comic Con (NYCC) surpassed San Diego Comic-Con's attendance numbers to become the largest pop culture convention in America. Held in October each year, NYCC is a celebration of all things geek.[4] The four-day event boasts a giant exhibitor hall, hundreds of panels and events programming, an Artist Alley featuring comic book artist guests, hundreds of celebrity guests, and a costume contest known as the NYCC Eastern Championships of Cosplay, which is the "largest and most prestigious costume contest on the East coast." The winner of this contest moves on to the final round at the C2E2 convention in Chicago to compete for the C2E2 Crown Championship of Cosplay.[5] NYCC is organized by ReedPop Events, which is also responsible for organizing twenty-five other well-known comic book, pop culture, gaming, and miscellaneous conventions, including the PAX cons, Emerald City Comic Con, C2E2, Special Edition NYC, Book Con, and more.

2. Comic-Con International: San Diego

http://www.comic-con.org
Date: July
Location: San Diego, CA
Number of Attendees: 130,000+
Type of Event: Comic book and pop culture convention
How Many Days: 4
Date of Origin: 1970

The long-standing champion of North American pop culture events, San Diego Comic-Con vies annually with NYCC for hosting the largest and most well-attended comic book and popular culture convention in North America. This well-known event hosts the prestigious Will Eisner Comic Industry Awards annually, along with hosting a 460,000-square-foot exhibit hall, over seven hundred programming events, thousands of artists and celebrity guests, and a Masquerade costume competition. The first three-day San Diego Comic-Con event in 1970 featured guests Ray Bradbury, Jack Kirby, and A. E. van Vogt and drew over three hundred attendees to the hotel basement space.[6]

3. Fan Expo Canada

http://fanexpocanada.com
Date: August
Location: Toronto, Canada
Number of Attendees: 127,000
Type of Event: Pop culture convention
How Many Days: 4
Date of Origin: 1994[7]

The largest pop culture convention in Canada, Pop Expo Canada is a four-day event that takes place in the sprawling 750,000-square-foot Metro Toronto Convention Centre space. Known as *the* "Comic Con" of Canada, this exciting event is packed with panels, programming, guests, and over one thousand exhibitors pertinent to comics, sci-fi, horror, anime, and gaming.[8]

4. Calgary Comic and Entertainment Expo

http://www.calgaryexpo.com
Date: April

Location: Calgary, Canada
Number of Attendees: 102,000
Type of Event: Comic book and pop culture convention
How Many Days: 4
Date of Origin: 2006

Held at the Stampede Park Grounds each April, this four-day event has become the second-largest pop culture convention in Canada. Featuring science fiction, comic books, fantasy, horror, pop culture, and animation programming, with panels located throughout the park, as well as an exhibit hall in the BMO Convention Centre, celebrity guests, and more, this con is a celebration of all things pop culture.[9]

5. Denver Comic Con

http://denvercomiccon.com
Date: May
Location: Denver, CO
Number of Attendees: 86,500+[10]
Type of Event: Comic book and pop culture convention
How Many Days: 3
Date of Origin: 2012

The Denver Comic Con and Literary Conference was founded by the creators of the Comic Book Classroom and remains a family-friendly, education-centered convention. Comic Book Classroom has since changed its name to the Pop Culture Classroom (PCC)[11] and continues to host this successful event, providing over three hundred hours of educational programming, including a literary conference offering graduate credits; panels for sci-fi, fantasy, film, and Japanese animation fans; celebrity guests and artists, and more.[12]

6. MegaCon

http://megaconvention.com
Date: April
Location: Orlando, FL
Number of Attendees: 80,000+
Type of Event: Comic book and pop culture convention
How Many Days: 3
Date of Origin: 1993[13]

This Orlando-based pop culture convention caters to comic book, sci-fi, anime, fantasy, and gaming fans through programming, panels, celebrity guests, and even a Tattoo Festival offering geeky and horror tattoos.[14]

7. Anime Expo

http://www.anime-expo.org
Date: July
Location: Los Angeles, CA
Number of Attendees: 80,000
Type of Event: Anime convention

How Many Days: 4
Date of Origin: 1992

Organized by the nonprofit Society for the Promotion of Japanese Animation, Anime Expo (AX) is the largest anime con in North America.[15] The event features programming such as anime and manga industry panels, maid and butler cafés, fashion shows, academic programs consisting of lectures from comics and animation scholars, gaming stations, a cosplay masquerade, and cosplay photo sets similar to those found in Japanese cosplay venues.[16]

8. Emerald City Comic Con

http://emeraldcitycomicon.com
Date: End of March/early April
Location: Seattle, WA
Number of Attendees: 80,000[17]
Type of Event: Comic book and pop culture convention
How Many Days: 3
Date of Origin: 2003

This all-ages comic and pop culture event features programming and panels, gaming, workshops, an exhibitor floor, comic book artists, and celebrity guests, as well as an annual costume contest. The three-day con will expand to four days beginning in 2016[18] and is hosted at the Washington State Convention Center in Seattle, Washington.

9. Phoenix Comicon

http://phoenixcomicon.com
Date: 2002
Location: Phoenix, AZ
Number of Attendees: 77,000+
Type of Event: Comic book and pop culture convention
How Many Days: 4
Date of Origin: 2002

Originally known as the Phoenix Cactus Comicon in 2002, which was one day and six hours long, this multigenre pop culture event has grown into a four-day happening. It provides programming, artists, and celebrity guests appealing to the comic book, anime, horror, sci-fi, fantasy, and gaming communities.[19]

10. PAX Prime and PAX East

http://prime.paxsite.com/
http://east.paxsite.com/
Date: August/September and March
Location: Seattle, WA/Boston, MA
Number of Attendees: 70,000+
Type of Event: Gaming convention
How Many Days: 4 (PAX Prime)/3 (PAX East)
Date of Origin: 2004[20]

The Penny Arcade Expo (PAX) Prime in Seattle and PAX East in Boston are two of the largest gaming events in North America. This convention features an exhibit hall with game publishers and developers previewing unreleased games and hardware, a console freeplay area, concerts, panels, a PC area, tabletop gaming section, and a handheld lounge. The folks who run this convention also organize PAX South in San Antonio, Texas; PAX Aus in Melbourne, Australia; and PAX Dev, a two-day preconference for game developers before the PAX Prime event.[21]

11. C2E2: Chicago Comic & Entertainment Expo

http://www.c2e2.com
Date: April
Location: Chicago
Number of Attendees: 63,000+[22]
Type of Event: Pop culture convention
How Many Days: 3
Date of Origin: 2010
   A multigenre event dedicated to all things pop culture, including video games, film, TV, comic books, anime, and more. Jam-packed with panels and programming, celebrity and artist guests, and film screenings, this event hosts the annual C2E2 Crown Championships of Cosplay—"the largest and most prestigious cosplay competition in the United States."[23]

12. Comic-Con International Presents WonderCon Anaheim

http://www.comic-con.org/wca
Date: April
Location: Anaheim, CA
Number of Attendees: 60,000[24]
Type of Event: Comic book and pop culture convention
How Many Days: 3
Date of Origin: 1987
   WonderCon is the sister event to San Diego Comic-Con and features programming and guests catering to the comic book, film, TV, and sci-fi communities. The event also hosts the annual Robert A. Heinlein Memorial Blood Drive and the International Children's Film Festival, as well as a masquerade and special screenings of Japanese animation films.[25]

13. Wizard World Chicago

http://www.wizardworld.com/chicago.html
Date: August
Location: Chicago, IL
Number of Attendees: 58,000
Type of Event: Pop culture convention
How Many Days: 4
Date of Origin: 1997
   Wizard Entertainment hosts nearly thirty comic con events across the country, including Wizard World Chicago. They feature pop culture celebrities and panel programming, as well as comic book artists and vendors.[26]

14. DragonCon

http://www.dragoncon.org
Date: Labor Day Weekend
Location: Atlanta, GA
Number of Attendees: 57,000+[27]
Type of Event: Pop culture convention
How Many Days: 4
Date of Origin: 1987

DragonCon is a unique pop culture convention steeped in science fiction, fantasy, comics, art, and gaming. It organizes events such as wrestling, burlesque revues, puppet slams, belly dance and Tai Chi workshops, and LARPing (live action role playing). Programming is divided into thirty-eight programming tracks,[28] including three thousand hours of comic book, costuming, film, and gaming panels and events spanning the four-day convention.[29] Programming tracks range from horror and animation to J. R. R. Tolkien's Middle-earth, *Star Wars*, urban gaming, and the Whedonverse. The Annual DragonCon Parade down Peachtree Street draws over 1,800 participants each year.[30] The event runs an annual blood drive within the con, which boasted nearly three thousand donors in 2014. Each year the con chooses a charity to which it matches donations, and it has raised over $311,000 for its featured charities since 2005.[31]

15. Otakon

http://www.otakon.com
Date: July
Location: Baltimore, MD
Number of Attendees: 33,000+
Type of Event: Anime convention
How Many Days: 3
Date of Origin: 1993

Otakon, a combination of the words *convention* and *otaku*, is the second-largest North American anime convention. It features programming such as panels and workshops, celebrity guests such as voice actors and anime artists, LARPing, and a DJ dance party.[32]

DISCOVERING CONVENTIONS

While these events are some of the most popular, this list is by no means exhaustive. There are hundreds more across North America and the world. How do you find out about comic cons, anime cons, and other events in your area? One of the best ways is to attend one and keep your eyes open for organizers advertising upcoming conventions that will be held nearby. A great way to find out about local events is to join your local cosplay community online, which will be discussed next. And finally, for major conventions, you can explore these online directories:

- Upcoming Cons: http://www.upcomingcons.com
- Convention Scene: http://www.conventionscene.com

LOCAL EVENTS

Aside from major conventions, there are many other opportunities for cosplaying that happen at the local level. These cosplay events might be a cosplay party, a themed photo shoot, a cosplay day in the park, a cosplay picnic, or even a cosplay subway ride! Alternatively, there may be events happening for occasions such as Free Comic Book Day, which occurs annually on the first Saturday in May, or to celebrate International Cosplay Day, which falls on the last Saturday of August annually. How do you find out about these smaller, local events? And how can libraries list their own and/or partner with organizers of existing area gatherings? By joining your local cosplay community.

CONNECTING WITH THE COSPLAY COMMUNITY

The best way to connect with and keep your finger on the pulse of what's happening in your local cosplay scene is to look for their groups and hangouts online. Facebook hosts a robust community of cosplayers who are very active in groups dedicated to costume creation and design, prop making, cosplay photography, cosplay commissions, and more. General groups are great for tips and advice and announcements of large events, while geographic groups on both Facebook and Meetup.com can help you narrow your focus to your area's community. Similarly, event-specific groups are a great platform to connect with cosplayers who will be attending large conventions in your area. Savvy librarians will partner with these groups to piggyback on the popularity of established cons and get the word out about their own events.

General Facebook Groups

Facebook is an excellent resource for cosplay groups, which provide advice and networking opportunities within the larger cosplay community. Here are just a sample of these groups. It is important to note that most groups will provide rules of conduct in the "About" section on the right-hand side of their page. This is where you can find out what is appropriate to post to that group's wall and what will be considered spam. When in doubt, you can always message the administrator(s) of the group, who can be found by clicking "Members" and then changing the default criteria to search by "Admins" rather than by "All Members" by changing the drop-down filter.

- Cosplay
  - https://www.facebook.com/groups/Cosplaywithme
  - 21,776 members
- Cosplay
  - https://www.facebook.com/groups/6170478997/
  - 16,747 members
- Cosplay- It Unites Us!
  - https://www.facebook.com/groups/132852926748096/
  - 9,807 members
- Cosplay for Sale!
  - https://www.facebook.com/groups/cosplay.for.sale
  - 7,312 members

- Cosplay Commissions
  - https://www.facebook.com/groups/cosplaycommissions
  - 6,484 members
- Cosplay Exchange
  - https://www.facebook.com/groups/cosplayexchange
  - 5,014 members
- Cosplayer Nation
  - https://www.facebook.com/groups/CosplayerNation
  - 4,947 members
- Cosplayers & Photographers
  - https://www.facebook.com/groups/513640968663493/
  - 4,713 members
- Cosplay Photography Discussion Group
  - https://www.facebook.com/groups/cosplayphotogs/?ref=br_rs
  - 3,996 members
- Cosplay Help and Advice
  - https://www.facebook.com/groups/403778536351822
  - 2,558 members
- Cosplay on a Budget
  - https://www.facebook.com/groups/CosplayOnaBudget/
  - 1,466 members
- Cosplay Support
  - https://www.facebook.com/groups/508737602592345
  - 659 members

Geographic/Local Groups

To find local groups, your best bet is to search Meetup.com not only for cosplay but for individual fandoms such as *Star Trek*, *Star Wars*, and *Doctor Who*, as well as genres such as sci-fi, horror, fantasy, and so on. You can also do the same on Facebook and look for groups to join. Here are a few examples:

- NY SciFi & Fantasy Meetup
  - http://www.meetup.com/NYSciFi-Fantasy
  - 2,393 members
- NY Cosplayer/Costumer Network & East/West Coast Friends!
  - https://www.facebook.com/groups/nycpn14/
  - 591 members
- New York Cosplayer Network! Meetup
  - http://www.meetup.com/cosplayasrule
  - 497 members
- Cosplay NY
  - https://www.facebook.com/groups/27265640806
  - 464 members
- South Carolina Cosplayers
  - https://www.facebook.com/groups/SCcosplay/
  - 458 members

- DC Cosplayers East (see figure 9 for a group photo)
  - https://www.facebook.com/groups/justiceleaguejusticesociety
  - 220 members

Event-Specific Groups

Most major conventions and occasions have a respective Facebook group or page. They may also have smaller pages dedicated to cosplayers who will be attending the con. It is important to realize that many cosplayers travel around the country and the world in order to attend different conventions and events. Some of these event-specific groups will be open to anyone who wants to join, while others will be invite-only and may be troupes of cosplayers who are planning to meet up at the event, each in a themed group cosplay that is planned months ahead of time. Here are some examples:

- Dragon*Con Cosplayers
  - https://www.facebook.com/groups/155203131258950
  - 2,155 members
- New York Comic Con NYCC + New York Anime Festival NYAF
  - https://www.facebook.com/groups/103870436382629/
  - 3,837 members
- International Cosplay Day
  - https://www.facebook.com/groups/InternationalCosplayDayGroup
  - 5,106 members
- Greek Mythology at Dragon*Con (see figure 10 for a group photo)
  - https://www.facebook.com/groups/135344613345
  - 143 members
- Rockabilly X-Men for DragonCon 2015
  - https://www.facebook.com/groups/582796875164827
  - 20 members

Format-Specific Groups

There are also many Facebook groups dedicated to working with specific materials or techniques. These are excellent places to find advice for sewing and designing costumes and building props, as well as project ideas for library cosplay events. These are just a few:

- Costuming and Props Think Tank Forum for Sci-Fi and All Genres
  - https://www.facebook.com/groups/351523644916186
  - 21,094 members
- The Replica Prop Forum
  - https://www.facebook.com/groups/therpf
  - 17,109 members
- United Prop Builders
  - https://www.facebook.com/groups/452833288060861
  - 5,977 members
- Sewing for Steampunk and Cosplay
  - https://www.facebook.com/groups/sewingforsteampunk
  - 5,309 members

Genre-Specific Groups

There are also many Facebook groups dedicated to particular fandoms and genres. If you are planning a fandom-related event in your library, you might join these types of communities as resources. Here are a few examples:

- Anime Fever—Manga, Art, Cosplay, and Shows
  - https://www.facebook.com/groups/AnimeFevers
  - 39,398 members
- *Star Trek* Cosplay
  - https://www.facebook.com/groups/StarTrekCosplay/
  - 1,014 members
- Marvel Cosplay International
  - https://www.facebook.com/groups/1394438210814836
  - 1,685 members

CHARITY AND COSPLAY

Cosplayers love to help out with charities by making special appearances at events, hospitals, charity auctions and fund-raisers, and so on. While most individuals are quick to respond to a call on Facebook to help out nonprofits and other good causes, there are also some organizations that have dedicated themselves to charity work. These are great groups to know about while seeking partnerships for library events. The most well-known organization is the 501st Legion, a volunteer organization of *Star Wars* costume enthusiasts. Here are just a few charitable cosplay organizations:

- 501st Legion
  - http://www.501st.com
  - https://www.facebook.com/The501stLegion
- Cosplay 4 Charity
  - http://www.cosplay4charity.be/index.html
  - https://www.facebook.com/Cosplay4Charity
- Cosplay for a Cause
  - http://cosplayforacause.com/
  - https://www.facebook.com/CosplayforACause
- Heroes Alliance
  - http://www.heroesalliance.org
  - https://www.facebook.com/HeroesAlliance.org

COSPLAY WEBSITES AND MAGAZINES

There are many websites, online magazines, and even print magazines that feature cosplay sections or dedicate themselves wholly to the hobby. These outlets are important for cosplayers to know about so that they can see the top cosplays from various conventions, find out about and follow popular cosplayers, and submit their own photographs to those publications that accept submissions. Here are just a few cosplay-related magazines and websites; for a more comprehensive list, see "Must-Have Cosplay Resources" at the end of this book.

- *Cosplay Culture* magazine
  - http://cosplayculturemagazine.com/print-magazine
- *Geeks Are Sexy*
  - http://www.geeksaresexy.net
- *Generate: A Cosplay Magazine*
  - https://www.facebook.com/GenerateACM
- *We Rise Mag*
  - http://www.werisemag.com
- Women of Comic Book Cosplay
  - https://www.facebook.com/comicbookcosplay

COSPLAY PHOTOGRAPHY

Cosplay photography is a unique photography niche. There are many photographers who specialize in taking pictures of cosplayers, groups, and costumed events. These experts understand how to organize group, fandom-related photo shoots; subdivide large groups into related character factions; highlight costume elements and props; organize action poses; and hide armor fixtures, straps, and other distractions. See appendix D, "Photographers Directory," for a list of cosplay photographers by state.

NOTES

1. Jayme Rebecca Taylor, "Convention Cosplay: Subversive Potential in Anime Fandom" (master's thesis, University of British Columbia, 2009), 7.
2. Gary Berman, e-mail message to author, April 2, 2015.
3. Heidi MacDonald, "What Are the Biggest Comic-Cons in North America?" *PWxyz*, June 19, 2013, http://blogs.publishersweekly.com/blogs/PWxyz/2013/06/19/what-are-the-biggest-comic-cons-in-north-america/.
4. "NYCC Fan FAQs," New York Comic Con, accessed February 27, 2015, http://www.newyorkcomiccon.com/About/NYCC-Fan-FAQs/.
5. "NYCC Eastern Championships of Cosplay," New York Comic Con, accessed February 27, 2015, http://www.newyorkcomiccon.com/Events/NYCC-Eastern-Championships-of-Cosplay/.
6. "About," Comic-Con International: San Diego, accessed January 20, 2015, http://www.comic-con.org/about.
7. "Fan Expo Canada," *Wikipedia*, accessed February 27, 2015, http://en.wikipedia.org/wiki/Fan_Expo_Canada.
8. "About Us," Fan Expo Canada, accessed February 27, 2015, http://fanexpocanada.com/about-us/.
9. "Calgary Comic and Entertainment Expo," *Wikipedia*, accessed April 22, 2015, http://en.wikipedia.org/wiki/Calgary_Comic_and_Entertainment_Expo.
10. "What We're About," Denver Comic Con, accessed April 20, 2015, http://denvercomiccon.com/about/.
11. "Our Story," Denver Comic Con, accessed April 20, 2015, http://denvercomiccon.com/history/.
12. "What We're About," Denver Comic Con.
13. "MegaCon," *Wikipedia*, accessed April 22, 2015, http://en.wikipedia.org/wiki/MegaCon.

14. "Tattoo Pavilion," MegaCon, accessed April 22, 2015, http://megaconvention.com/tattoo-pavilion-2/.

15. "Anime Expo," *Wikipedia*, accessed April 22, 2015, http://en.wikipedia.org/wiki/Anime_Expo.

16. Anime Expo website, accessed April 22, 2015, http://www.anime-expo.org/.

17. ECCC Press Relations, e-mail message to author, April 2, 2015.

18. Andrea D., "ECCC Expands to Four Days in 2016," Emerald City Comic Con, March 27, 2015, http://emeraldcitycomicon.com/news/.

19. "Phoenix Comicon," *Wikipedia*, accessed April 22, 2015, http://en.wikipedia.org/wiki/Phoenix_Comicon.

20. "Penny Arcade Expo," *Wikipedia*, accessed April 22, 2015, http://en.wikipedia.org/wiki/Penny_Arcade_Expo.

21. "What Is PAX," PAX Prime, accessed April 22, 2015, http://prime.paxsite.com/what-is-pax.

22. "Chicago Comic & Entertainment Expo C2E2 2015 Sales Kit," Chicago Comic & Entertainment Expo, accessed April 20, 2015, http://www.c2e2.com/rna/rna_c2e2_v2/documents/2014/2015-c2e2-sales-kit.pdf?v=635375819658874101.

23. "C2E2 Crown Championships of Cosplay," Chicago Comic & Entertainment Expo, accessed April 20, 2015, http://www.c2e2.com/Events/Events-A-H/C2E2-Crown-Championships-of-Cosplay/.

24. "WonderCon," *Wikipedia*, accessed April 20, 2015, http://en.wikipedia.org/wiki/WonderCon.

25. Comic-Con International Presents WonderCon Anaheim 2015 website, accessed April 22, 2015, http://www.comic-con.org/wca/.

26. "Wizard Entertainment," *Wikipedia*, accessed April 20, 2015, http://en.wikipedia.org/wiki/Wizard_Entertainment#Conventions.

27. "Dragon Con 2014 Fact Sheet," DragonCon Media Relations, accessed April 20, 2015, http://mediarelations.dragoncon.org/DragonConFactSheet2014.pdf.

28. "Fan Tracks," DragonCon, accessed April 20, 2015, http://www.dragoncon.org/?q=fan-tracks-view.

29. "Dragon Con 2014 Fact Sheet," DragonCon Media Relations.

30. "History," DragonCon, accessed April 22, 2015, http://www.dragoncon.org/?q=history.

31. "Dragon Con 2014 Fact Sheet," DragonCon Media Relations.

32. "Otakon," *Wikipedia*, accessed April 20, 2015, http://en.wikipedia.org/wiki/Otakon.

4

Cosfamous

Although cosplay is simply a fun pastime for most, there are some cosplayers who have become recognized and well known for their costumes, armor, and prop creations; they have become "cosfamous." These cosplayers make their living from this creative hobby. They make guest appearances at comic and pop culture conventions and are sought after to judge cosplay contests at these events. They also sell signed photos, posters, and calendars, as well as books they have written on costume and prop-making techniques, and may even have their own line of merchandise. They are commissioned to cosplay as video game and other characters, design costumes and props for sale, and even make television appearances.

The 2013–2014 SyFy channel original series *Heroes of Cosplay* was a two-season reality TV show featuring cosplayers on the contest and competition circuit. Season 1 alone was watched by over one million viewers. The show received quite a bit of criticism from the cosplay community because it portrayed cosplayers as fiercely competitive creators who were less interested in the love of the hobby than with winning contests, which is quite far from the truth for most cosplayers, who create their costumes in order to express their fandom and be a part of the community.[1]

There are numerous cosplayers who enjoy incredible popularity and success from creating costumes in many different genres, including comic books, video games, anime, and more. Here are just ten examples of cosplayers who are well known at conventions and beyond.

COSFAMOUS COSPLAYERS

1. Alodia Gosiengfiao

https://www.facebook.com/AlodiaGosiengfiao
4,975,964 Facebook likes

Alodia Gosiengfiao is a Filipina cosplayer and model based in Manila, Philippines, and Tokyo. She has been cosplaying since 2003 at the age of fifteen and has made numerous appearances at conventions, cosplaying more than forty different video game, film, and anime characters. She has been hired by many companies in the Philippines to endorse their products and has been featured in newspapers, magazines, and TV shows. *UNO* magazine has named her one of the "most influential women in the Philippines."[2]

2. Jessica Nigri

https://www.facebook.com/OfficialJessicaNigri
2,698,663 Facebook likes

Jessica Nigri is an American cosplayer who has been cosplaying since 2009. She has been an official spokesperson for numerous comic book series and video games, including *Lollipop Chainsaw* and *Assassin's Creed IV: Black Flag*. She has also been an interviewer for many media outlets and a spokesmodel at various conventions.[3]

3. Yaya Han

https://www.facebook.com/yayacosplay
1,360,887 Facebook likes

One of the world's most well-known cosplayers, Yaya Han is an American cosplayer who has built a successful business out of cosplaying. She has won numerous awards for her elaborate costumes and has been invited to more than one hundred conventions to perform, appear as a guest, and judge cosplay contests. She has her own line of wigs, T-shirts, and cosplay accessories such as wings, ears, and unicorn horns.[4] She has made television appearances on SyFy's *Heroes of Cosplay* as well as the TBS reality show *King of the Nerds*.[5]

4. Nicole Marie Jean

https://www.facebook.com/NicoleMarieJeanPage
936,873 Facebook likes

A San Diego–based cosplayer, Nicole Marie Jean has been cosplaying since 2011. She has won numerous awards and contests for her nearly sixty-five costumes and is most well known for her portrayal of Bane, the *Batman* villain.[6]

5. Stella Chuu

https://www.facebook.com/stellachuuuuu
516,492 Facebook likes

Stella Chuu is a New York–based cosplayer and burlesque performer. She has been cosplaying since 2011 and has appeared in many media outlets and interviews.[7]

6. Monika Lee

https://www.facebook.com/London2191Cosplay
338,561 Facebook likes

Monika Lee started cosplaying at the age of thirteen and has been featured by many media outlets such as the Associated Press, IGN, and Game Informer. She is very well known for her portrayal of Little Sister from the BioShock video game series. A senior at the Georgia Institute of Technology studying industrial design, Monika manages to attend many conventions a year and has appeared on SyFy's *Heroes of Cosplay*.[8]

7. Ivy Doomkitty

https://www.facebook.com/ivydoomkittyivy
297,958 Facebook likes

A Los Angeles–based cosplayer, Ivy Doomkitty has been a guest, panelist, and host at numerous conventions. She was also a guest judge for cosplay contests on Syfy's *Heroes of Cosplay*. She is a spokesperson for positive body image in cosplay and encourages potential cosplayers to participate regardless of their body shape, size, ethnicity, or sexual orientation[9] through her panel discussions, such as her recent talk "Body Confidence and Positivity in Cosplay" at WonderCon Anaheim 2015.[10]

8. Maridah

https://www.facebook.com/MaridahCosplay
229,509 Facebook likes

Rachel Lynn, aka Maridah,[11] is a Los Angeles–based cosplayer best known for her Saber cosplay from *Fate Stay Night*. She has been cosplaying since she was seventeen years old in 2001. She is a frequent guest of honor at anime conventions, a Crunchyroll ambassador, and has appeared in a number of media outlets.[12]

9. Vampy

https://www.facebook.com/VAMPYBITME
225,193 Facebook likes

An American cosplayer of Vietnamese descent, Linda Le, aka Vampy, has a business degree from San Jose State University. Most well known for her portrayal of Psylocke from *X-Men*, Vampy has collaborated with numerous artists and entertainment companies, has attended more than two hundred conventions, and has been written about by many media outlets.[13]

10. Kamui Cosplay

https://www.facebook.com/KamuiCos
204,129 Facebook likes

Born in Angren, Uzbekistan, Svetlana Quindt, aka Kamui Cosplay, is a Germany-based cosplayer famed for her intricate armor builds and props. She offers many tutorials, walkthrough videos, and several books to teach others how to create, paint, and fasten their own armor, as well as build prop weapons and accessories.[14] See figures 2, 20, and 30 for examples of her work.

COSPLAY AND FANDOM GROUPS

In addition to individual cosplayers, there are many troupes of cosplayers who have organized themselves around a particular theme or fandom. Most notable are the many *Star Wars*, *Star Trek*, and *Ghostbusters* cosplay groups. These groups meet and discuss costume ideas and the particular television show, film, or video game that inspires them, as well socialize with others who share a common interest. Many of these groups also undertake charitable works as a part of their mission. These organized groups are very helpful to know about when planning a library comic con or other cosplay-related event, especially if you are looking for featured guests to invite.

The Harry Potter Alliance

http://thehpalliance.org

There are many groups dedicated to the fandom of *Harry Potter*, but the most notable is a social change organization created in 2005 called the Harry Potter Alliance, which has over 275 chapters in 43 U.S. states and 25 countries.[15] Individual chapters such as the Rocky Mountain Muggles (https://www.facebook.com/TheRockyMountainMuggles) volunteer their time to appear at events and coordinate efforts in order to support the organization's larger goals of community activism. Founded by Andrew Slack and the wizard rock band Harry and the Potters,[16] they run an annual Accio Books campaign to help build libraries in Rwanda and other disadvantaged areas, as well as partner with many other charities and organizations to do good work.[17]

Browncoats—*Firefly* Fandom

Fans of Joss Whedon's *Firefly* TV series are known as Browncoats, named after the uniforms worn by the members of the resistance who opposed the Alliance government during the Unification War.[18] Three organized cosplay groups exist, which are each nonprofit organizations that strive to promote *Firefly* fandom through charitable works:

- Austin Browncoats: http://www.austinbrowncoats.com
- California Browncoats: http://www.californiabrowncoats.org
- Southeastern Browncoats: http://www.southeasternbrowncoats.com

Ghostbusters

There are many cosplay groups dedicated to creating costumes and props based on the *Ghostbusters* films. If you conduct a search for your city or state plus the term "Ghostbusters" on Facebook, you will most likely find a nearby troupe, such as:

- Alabama Ghostbusters: https://www.facebook.com/alabamaghostbusters
- Indiana Ghostbusters: Jasper District: https://www.facebook.com/IN.GBJasper
- Sacramento Ghostbusters: https://www.facebook.com/sacghostbusters
- The Ghostbusters of New Hampshire: https://www.facebook.com/GhostbustersofNew Hampshire
- The Real Tampa Bay Ghostbusters: https://www.facebook.com/realtampbayghostbusters (see figure 11 for a photo)

Star Wars

All three of these costuming organizations are very involved with volunteerism and charity, as well as with expressing their enthusiasm for the *Star Wars* films through cosplay and community, the largest and most well-known being the 501st Legion.

- 501st Legion: Vader's Fist: http://www.501st.com
- The Rebel Legion: http://www.rebellegion.com
- Empire Saber Guild: http://empiresaberguild.com

The 1701st Fleet—Star Trek Fandom

https://www.facebook.com/The1701stFleet

The 1701st Fleet is an international *Star Trek* cosplay and fan association with many chapters, the largest of which is the *U.S.S. Navras* at https://www.facebook.com/ussnavras. The group describes themselves as the Star Trek version of the 501st Legion since they are also an all-volunteer organization that makes public appearances to raise awareness and funds for charities.[19]

NOTES

1. "*Heroes of Cosplay*," *Wikipedia*, accessed April 20, 2015, http://en.wikipedia.org/wiki/Heroes_of_Cosplay.

2. "About Alodia Gosiengfiao," Facebook, accessed April 20, 2015, https://www.facebook.com/AlodiaGosiengfiao/info.

3. "Jessica Nigri," *Wikipedia*, accessed April 20, 2015, http://en.wikipedia.org/wiki/Jessica_Nigri.

4. "Yaya Han," Facebook, accessed April 21, 2015, https://www.facebook.com/yayacosplay.

5. "Yaya Han," *Wikipedia*, accessed April 20, 2015, http://en.wikipedia.org/wiki/Yaya_Han.

6. "About Nicole Marie Jean," Facebook, accessed April 21, 2015, https://www.facebook.com/NicoleMarieJeanPage/info.

7. "About Stella Chuu," Facebook, accessed April 21, 2015, https://www.facebook.com/stellachuuuuu/info.

8. "About Monika Lee," Facebook, accessed April 21, 2015, https://www.facebook.com/London-2191Cosplay/info.

9. "About Ivy Doomkitty," Facebook, accessed April 21, 2015, https://www.facebook.com/ivydoomkittyivy/info.

10. "Schedule," WonderCon Anaheim, accessed April 21, 2015, https://wonderconanaheim2015.sched.org/event/f1d2382d7518f413edd0377447b18d61#.VTgPMnv-wXs.

11. "About Maridah," Maridah.com, accessed April 20, 2015, http://www.maridah.com/about.html.

12. "About Maridah," Facebook, accessed April 20, 2015 https://www.facebook.com/MaridahCosplay/info.

13. "Linda Le," *Wikipedia*, accessed April 20, 2015, http://en.wikipedia.org/wiki/Linda_Le.

14. "About Me," KamuiCosplay.com, accessed April 20, 2015, http://www.kamuicosplay.com/press/.

15. "Success Stories," The Harry Potter Alliance, accessed April 20, 2015, http://thehpalliance.org/what-we-do/success-stories/.

16. "Harry Potter Alliance," *Wikipedia*, accessed April 22, 2015, http://en.wikipedia.org/wiki/Harry_Potter_Alliance.

17. "Success Stories," The Harry Potter Alliance.

18. "Browncoat," *Wikipedia*, accessed April 22, 2015, http://en.wikipedia.org/wiki/Browncoat.

19. "About *U.S.S. Navras*," Facebook, accessed April 22, 2015, https://www.facebook.com/ussnavras/info.

5

Libraries Embracing Cosplay

Many libraries have started to host cosplay-related events in their libraries, including cosplay days, lock-ins, comic cons, anime cons, and more. These events are proving to be extremely well attended and popular with the local community and don't cost nearly as much as you'd think! No matter what size budget your library has, you too can host one of these types of events. Here are some examples of libraries who are embracing cosplay through their programming.

MID-PINELLAS COMIC AND MAKER CON 2014[1]

St. Petersburg College and the Seminole Community Library
https://www.facebook.com/PCMCon
Date: August 9, 2014
Cost of the Event: $500
How Many Attendees: 3,500
Estimated Number of Cosplayers: 300

Chad Mairn, information services librarian and Innovation Lab manager at St. Petersburg College, organized the library's first Mid-Pinellas Comic and Maker Con in conjunction with the Seminole Community Library in less than six weeks and on a shoestring budget. Chad partnered with Greg Plantamura, who helped organize the Clearwater Library Comic Con a few months prior. They reached out to local comic book, gaming, and cosplay stores, which were all invaluable resources. This was an all-ages, family-friendly event, and it received rave reviews from the postevent survey and via the event's Facebook page. Chad and his team, which also included Mike Bryan and Jill Storm from the library, the campus provost Dr. Jim Olliver, and a plethora of security and facilities staff, hoped that the event would be attended by 400 to 600 people based on the Clearwater Library event; however, this first comic con turned out to be wildly popular, attracting a total of 3,500 people. When asked why he decided to organize such an event, Chad responded,

> Any event that can give the library more visibility is a good thing. Comic books, anime, etc., are literature. They are art too! Shining a light on that fact is important. I think librarians and teachers

should be sharing all kinds of materials, not just "academic" or "classic" literature, to inspire people and to get them excited about reading, thinking, dreaming, and making. Also, I have been wanting to do a comic con with an additional maker component for a while, but it wasn't until Greg Plantamura, who helped organize the Clearwater Public Library Comic Con, reached out to me to see if my college library would be interested in doing something similar. That was the spark that started the fire.

The event featured celebrity guests such as comic artist Austin Janowsky, cosplay performers such as the Tampa Spider-Man and the Real Tampa Bay Ghostbusters, and the 501st Legion *Star Wars* cosplay troupe. The one-day con was filled with fun activities such as face painting, a gaming tournament organized by a local gaming organization, and a TARDIS (Doctor Who's time-traveling police box) for photos. Con-goers had the opportunity to learn about the planning and makeup effects of Busch Gardens' Howl-O-Scream Halloween event in a behind-the-scenes panel, as well as attend other panel discussions on cosplay and costuming, *Doctor Who*, horror movies, and superheroines and pop culture. The con also featured a video game tournament, which was projected onto large screens across the library so that people entering the con could see the event.

The event hosted costume contests for both kids and adults, as well as a character voice sound-alike contest in which participants had a chance to show off their impressions. Since many con-goers were in costume, they ended up with some humorous combinations, such as Spider-Man impersonating Darth Vader. The costume contests were so successful that the library will plan more for next year and move them to a larger area where they don't block traffic. The con had five food trucks serving different types of cuisine for con-goers and plenty of local comic book, hobby, and video game shops and local makers participating as exhibitors. While the event didn't charge exhibitors to participate, many of the vendors donated prizes and giveaways for the event, such as tickets to the Busch Gardens' Howl-O-Scream Halloween attraction and Legoland. Next year the staff will allow vendors to sell items at the con. Library staff had thought that since the library is a nonprofit organization that vendors were prohibited from selling items, but they have since learned that the library is indeed able to allow this. With regard to this, the staff are considering whether they will charge vendors for participation next year or ask them for a nominal donation in order to fund the event. The next Mid-Pinellas Comic and Maker Con, now called the Pinellas Comic and Maker Con, will be held on October 17, 2015, and the staff expect a large turnout this year as well.

AFTER HOURS TEEN FANDOM EVENT[2]

Library: ELANCO Library
https://www.facebook.com/pages/ELANCO-Library-Teens/415155415829
Date: Ongoing, every other month
Cost of the Event: $60
How Many Attendees: 40
Estimated Number of Cosplayers: 40

Heather Warren Smith, youth services librarian at ELANCO Library, has organized a bimonthly after-hours cosplay event for seventh through twelfth graders for the past two years. It is a locked event that is staffed by Heather, a second staff member, and two volunteers. Teens arrive in costume, dressed as their favorite character from a book, movie, TV show, or comic, at promptly 6:30 p.m. on a Saturday. At this time, half an hour is allotted for socializing and selfies, after which the activities begin. At these events, teens sing Japanese cartoon theme songs as well as pop hits during karaoke; express themselves artistically with coloring pages from fandoms such as *Doctor Who*, *Homestuck*, and *Percy Jackson*; play an endless trivia game for which the teens write the questions themselves; and have a cosplay contest with prizes given out for the categories: most authentic, most creative, and fan favorite.

During the final hour of the event, all but the emergency lights are switched off, and teens are given free rein to run around two floors of the library in costume, playing a game called Murder by Candlelight, an exciting form of tag made up of assigned murderers, survivors, and zombies, all of which must scream loudly when eliminated from the game. (See appendix A for the full rules.) At the conclusion of the event, the teens clean up after themselves and return all of the furniture to its rightful place. Heather, who at first misunderstood the teens' request to have a fandom event to be an interest in holding a *Phantom of the Opera* function, can't believe the success of the event, which has given teens, many of whom are homeschooled, a chance to socialize and build significant relationships with the library. "I believe that this program is helping them to become lifelong library users," Heather says, "and cosplay is what brought them here." See figures 12–14 for photos of these events.

TOSHOCON[3]

Library: Salt Lake County Library
https://www.facebook.com/Toshocon
Date: 2014
Cost of the Event: $2,500
How Many Attendees: 1,500
Estimated Number of Cosplayers: 60+

Carrie Rogers-Whitehead, senior librarian of teen services at the Salt Lake County Library, organizes the library's annual anime convention called ToshoCON, which began in 2013, for teens ages twelve to nineteen. Due to its popularity, the con has expanded into a two-day event featuring teen-run panels, an anime art contest, and a cosplay contest divided into skill levels and judged by local community members. The event also hosts a manga swap, craft activities, a vendor marketplace, a karaoke lounge, food trucks, and a dance. Additionally, a *Yu-Gi-Oh* gaming tournament is organized by a local gaming store, which also provides the prizes. The library charges vendors $50 for participation in the marketplace plus a $25 donation, which goes directly to the prizes awarded at the cosplay and anime-drawing contests. "The vendors weren't sure at first about participating since ToshoCON was a new event and it was for teens (who don't have as much money), but they found it worthwhile and most have returned in subsequent years," said Carrie.

According to Carrie, the event was planned to provide much-needed programming for teens:

> I had been doing a teen anime club for several years at the time I decided to start ToshoCON. I knew the interest was there, and those teens would be highly involved. I also knew the Utah geek community well and felt like there was a gap in programming for the younger ages, especially for teens. And there weren't many places that teens could plan the program, it was all adults, and the conventions cost money, which inhibited some teens from attending. And it was a hit with area teens. One of the most successful events was the anime art contest. We had almost 400 entries, and when you consider 1,600 participants, that's basically a quarter of teens participating in it! There's

never been an art contest in our library system that had nearly as many participants. We had to divide the art into 12–13, 14–15, 16–18 age groups and a digital category, and it was still a lot!

Although the library does invite some special guests, it is really the teens who take ownership of the event. It is the anime clubs from throughout the library system that coordinate the anime art contest, while other teens plan and speak on the panels. A three-hundred-plus-member teen Facebook group contributes to the event as well. One of the most surprising parts of running this event, according to Carrie, was the fact that the teens weren't really interested in having celebrity guests on the panels. She says, "They don't want to sit and hear adults talk, they want to speak on the panels along with their friends and have discussions." It is also surprising to note that the teens weren't interested in the professional photographer that the library had arranged. Instead, they wanted to take their own selfies. Most of the expenses for the event included printing and marketing the event, according to Carrie. Next year she will ask sponsors to donate bags for con-goers to use to carry all of their swag.

Carrie offers this advice to libraries considering hosting an anime con: "A mini convention is a great way to engage youth, reach out to the community and have fun! There are geeks and anime-lovers everywhere, and once you build it, they will come." See figure 15 for a photo of the event.

BURLINGTON COUNTY LIBRARY SYSTEM[4]

Library: Burlington County Library System
http://www.bcls.lib.nj.us
Date: 2014
Cost of the Event: $75 (approximately, for the lock-ins)
How Many Attendees: 20
Estimated Number of Cosplayers: 10

Kathleen Gruver, young adult librarian at the Burlington County Library System in Westampton, New Jersey, has been hosting cosplay-related programs in her library for years. One such program is an annual lock-in event, which often features a large cosplay component. Past themes have included superheroes, at which teens came dressed as their favorite hero from either Western or Japanese comics, and both pizza and Pocky were served. Participants took part in a cosplay parade and played games such as Extreme Trivia, which is a combination musical chairs plus trivia game. Kathleen hosted the event dressed as Wonder Woman, and another staffer dressed as Link from *Zelda*.

Another year's lock-in was *Hunger Games*–themed, at which teens divided into districts and held a tribute parade with decorated "chariots" made of book carts, crepe paper, and duct tape (see footage here: http://youtu.be/2vCvQx-Ihcc). Teens took part in a "Thriller" dance-off at one-year's zombie-themed lock-in, which also featured a digital-photo scavenger hunt around the library. At these lock-ins, teens play such ice-breaker games as a twenty-questions-style trivia game in which players must guess the identity of the character taped to their backs.

Kathleen notes that finances are often an issue with kids who may want to cosplay but cannot afford to. She offers this advice for these types of events: "You want to make sure there's something there for those kids who can't afford to cosplay but still love manga and comics." She goes on to say that kids will get very creative, such as coming as Light from *Death Note*, who only needs to carry a notebook for a costume, but that it's important to schedule activities that will also include those who aren't cosplaying.

The library has also hosted a February cosplay- and anime-themed party, which was a big hit with teens. Not only was there a cosplay parade but a *Naruto* ramen-eating contest using chopsticks! The toughest part of organizing these events according to Kathleen is "finding large amounts of Pocky."

CHIBICONN[5]

Library: Springfield City Library
http://www.springfieldlibrary.org/library/services/chibiconn-2014/
Date: November 2004, annually
Cost of the Event: $180
How Many Attendees: 80–125
Estimated Number of Cosplayers: 80

Sarah Hodge-Wetherbe, library associate at the Springfield City Library, organizes an annual two-day anime, comics, and pop culture convention called Chibiconn, which is always well attended by costumed teens. The event features guest speakers; panels on cosplay such as "Cosplay on a Budget," "Cosplay Culture," and "Last Minute Cosplay Fixes"; and featured cosplay groups such as the North East Ghostbusters Alliance: Taskforce Ecto, which made an appearance from New Hampshire and brought their Ghostbusters car with them. The event's costs lie mainly with speaker fees, which average about $150, and snacks at around $30.

According to Sarah, the second day of the event is always the most successful because of the cosplay programming and cosplay contest. Sarah is continually surprised by how amazing and creative the cosplayers' costumes are; one year a teen created an entire Iron Man suit for himself out of cardboard boxes! "One of my favorite parts of organizing these events is seeing how people take their favorite characters and make them their own," says Sarah.

The event evolves every year based on the feedback that library staff get from surveys passed out at the end of each day of the event. They've now moved away from the film festival aspect that they first incorporated and have integrated more hands-on activities and cosplay programming, as those items have been more popular. One activity that the library recently tried, a game called Cosplay Iron Chef, turned out to be very popular. Teams of teens were challenged to put together a costume from a box filled with random costuming supplies, such as curtains, duct tape, wigs, and so on. See Appendix A for full rules.

CHESTERFIELD PUBLIC LIBRARY COMIC-CON[6]

Library: Chesterfield Public Library
http://library.chesterfield.gov/events/comic-con
Date: March
Cost of the Event: $500
How Many Attendees: 2,150
Estimated Number of Cosplayers: 1,000+

Branch Managers Kareemah Hamdan and James Hudson, along with Library Specialist Kate Denwiddie, make up the organizational superteam behind the successful Chesterfield

Public Library Comic-Con in Midlothian, Virginia. Now in its third year, the event draws more than 2,100 attendees. The team originally decided to host their comic con as a promotional event in order to spotlight the comics and graphic novels collection that the library was developing. At the initial con, they had 1,500 items on display for patrons to peruse, of which 20 percent to 30 percent had been checked out by the end of the event. The organizers noted that kids (and adults) were leaving the library having snatched up an entire series each for loan.

"We have a comic con," says Kate, "but we do it in a library way." The library has interactive activities focusing on literacy and learning, such as a creative craft space. Staff also host jam-packed hands-on workshops with authors and illustrators teaching participants how to create their own comic strips, how to draw villains, and how to draw manga. For their next event, they're planning a boxcar rocket race in which participants will create their own rockets from repurposed materials found in the library. The event also features vendor and exhibitor tables, special guests such as comic book artists and the 501st Legion *Star Wars* cosplay group, anime screenings, and video games, as well as the HeroClix board game.

The entire staff dresses up in costume for the comic con and, according to James, cosplay has been by far the most popular part of the event. Kareemah adds, "You don't know how many people want to dress up until you throw one of these events!" The team notes that the cosplay contest requires the most amount of logistical planning of all of the activities since it's so popular, often drawing over 120 participants. If you are planning your own event, they suggest strategically placing the contest in an area that won't have heavy traffic and to plan a group photo of all of the participants in order to capture the moment. Additionally, if your librarians and staff will be judging the contest, they strongly recommend having a laptop handy to look up the contestant's costumes for comparison. For their contest, organizers purchased gift cards and a digital sketch tablet as prizes.

The staff tapped into the communications network of the local comic book store in order to spread the word about the event. They also partnered with a local art school that not only spread the word among students but designed the photo booth background for the event. Kate has been most surprised by the speed of success of the event, which was attended by thousands since the very first con. She says, "We knew it was a good idea, but it was surprising that it was such an instant success." James goes on to note: "It's been amazing to get such a large crowd for the amount of planning and preparation that goes into the event. This event boasts quadruple the attendance numbers of our other programs." Kareemah has been most surprised by the span of ages of patrons who come to the events, ranging from babies in strollers to seniors. This event brings people together from all backgrounds throughout the entire county who share similar interests. See figures 16 and 17 for photos of this event.

RAYMOND TIMBERLAND LIBRARY CUSTOM-MADE FOR COSPLAY[7]

Library: Raymond Timberland Library
 http://tinyurl.com/msu4nmd
Date: 2015
Cost of the Event: $0
How Many Attendees: 6–20
Estimated Number of Cosplayers: 6–20

Rachelle Martin is the youth services associate at the Raymond Timberland Library, a small branch library in a low-income, impoverished area with three school districts. She has partnered with the local Washington State University Master Quilters group, a 4-H club volunteer organization made up of retirees, in order to organize a truly unique event aimed at teens who want to cosplay but cannot afford to. At the event, each teen will be assigned their own seamstress and will meet with her three times at the library for fittings to collaboratively create their own cosplay costume. Rachelle met the quilters at a 4-H club event and originally approached them about helping with a thrift-store beginners cosplay event. Instead, the group offered to volunteer and fully fund all of the materials for this exciting cosplay project. Each teen will be expected to come to this under-twenty-one event with an idea of what/who they want to cosplay and work with their seamstress on the design. The teens' response has been that they are overwhelmed and excited and just can't believe that they will get to keep their costumes for free. According to Rachelle, this is shaping up to be one of the most popular events that the library has ever hosted.

HARRY POTTER YULE BALL[8]

Library: Salt Lake County Library
http://tinyurl.com/q8h75gv
Date: 2013, 2014, 2015
Cost of the Event: $1,500
How Many Attendees: 1,500
Estimated Number of Cosplayers: 1,500

Carrie Rogers-Whitehead, senior librarian of teen services at the Salt Lake County Library, organizes the library's annual Harry Potter Yule Ball every January for teens ages twelve to nineteen. This free event, now in its third year, is incredibly popular with teens, who are invited to come in costume or formal dress and enjoy a fantastical evening filled with activities, dancing, and a House Cup competition. Special guests such as the Rocky Mountain Muggles costume troupe perform, and Marshmallow the barn owl strikes a pose with wizards and muggles alike. Adventurous teens can take a turn holding a live python or tarantula brought by Creature Encounters. The enchanting event features fortune telling in a Divination Room, a Diagon Alley, a Platform 9¾ photo booth, free crafts such as wand making, and a McGonagall's Game Room, where teens can play board games. See figure 18 for a photo of the event.

FOREST PARK PUBLIC LIBRARY MINI COMIC CON[9]

Library: Forest Park Public Library
http://tinyurl.com/o65llcl
Date: January 10, 2015
Cost of the Event: $75–$250
How Many Attendees: 100 people
Estimated Number of Cosplayers: Only featured cosplayers

Martha Buehler, youth services librarian, helps organize the Forest Park Public Library's Mini Comic Con, which has been growing steadily in popularity over the past four years. Their event has featured local authors and comic book artists such as Neil Brideau, who draws kid-friendly comics; illustrator Yorli Huff (of the comic *Superhero Huff*); cosplay performers such as the Chicago Jedi group, who offered lightsaber lessons with Obi-Wan Kenobi; the

Midwest Tokusatsu, who donned *Power Rangers* costumes for the event; and the Midwest Garrison 501st Legion, another *Star Wars* cosplay group. The 501st Legion and the Chicago Jedi Group both made their appearances at the Mini Con for free, and organizers made donations to their supported charities in lieu of any payment.

This program, which started off as a teen event, has turned into an event for all ages, with panels, photo shoots, and interactive activities such as a "Make Your Own Cape and Mask" workshop. The event features face painting as well as vendors such as local comic book stores One Stop Comics and Defiant Comics, both of which have a strong presence at the convention. One of the most surprising parts of the Mini Con, according to Martha, is how young the kids are that turn out for the event. As a cosplayer and con-goer herself, Martha says, "You don't see too many small kids at the larger cons, the library's mini con is a way more accessible venue for younger comic fans since it's less overwhelming for them." The library's goal is to try to incorporate more cosplay programming going forward as the *Star Wars* cosplayers have been among the most successful parts of the Mini Con.

OTHER ORGANIZATIONS AND COSPLAY

New York Comic Con[10]
Event: NYCC Eastern Championships of Cosplay
http://www.newyorkcomiccon.com/Events/NYCC-Eastern-Championships-of-Cosplay/
Date: 2014
How Many Participants: 30

New York Comic Con (NYCC) is one of the largest comic book conventions in the world and has surpassed the well-known San Diego Comic-Con as of the 2014 event with 151,000 unique attendees. Their NYCC Eastern Championships of Cosplay is the most prestigious cosplay contest on the East Coast and is part of the Quest for the Crown global cosplay competition circuit. It is attended by an audience of thousands and viewed by many more around the world via the event's live stream. Brian Stephenson, brand marketing manager; Justin Flores, content and talent coordinator; and Chris Malico, international content coordinator, make up the ReedPop team that envisions and implements this extraordinary costume contest. Their goal is to elevate cosplay and lend it legitimacy by forming an official competition but also to create a kind of "Super Bowl" of cosplay, the winner of which moves on to challenge international winners in the final round at the Chicago Comic & Entertainment Expo (C2E2) Crown Championships of Cosplay.

This is a one-of-a-kind cosplay event that places talented costumers in front of a panel of judges who are experts in the field, including costume designers, trained seamstresses, armor-building experts, celebrities to judge stage presence, makeup artists, prop makers, and so on. Like other cosplay events, it also offers cosplayers a chance to meet other like-minded people and enjoy a sense of community. Organizers screen the applicant pool of about three hundred down to around thirty, who are then invited to compete on site at NYCC during the contest, which is divided into five categories: movies and TV, comic books, fantasy, anime, and video games. The competition is for ages eighteen and over or sixteen and over with parental consent. There is a prejudging round, where contestants meet with a panel of judges for three to five minutes off-stage in a room where the judges can see the fine detail of their costumes and ask questions about their garment. The cosplay contest rules specify that no purchased or unaltered materials can be used as part of the costume. If an article of clothing is purchased, it must be somehow customized for the contest. While other cosplay contests differ in their rules, this particular contest is for those who handcraft their costumes.

On the day of the event, contestants walk the stage and strike three poses while organizers switch between PowerPoint slides with their head-shot, name, and the character that they're representing, as well as a video of them walking the stage so that all two thousand people in the room can see them before they exit the stage. Other cons, such as Anime Expo, have even more elaborate displays, with cosplayers performing skits during their time on stage. The event is live-streamed to online viewers.

Organizers suggest that librarians who are planning cosplay contests should be prepared for all manner of surprises. During a previous contest at C2E2, the team had to warn a cosplayer with a seventeen-foot dragon costume *not* to breathe actual fire while on the stage. Additionally, the costume was so large that it couldn't fit through the doors, and while organizers were trying to figure out how it would get on stage, they lost track of the cosplayer and spent a harried preshow running around asking people if they'd seen a seventeen-foot dragon! At the NYCC Eastern Championships of Cosplay in 2014, a cosplayer's costume was so elaborate that she had to be pushed around on wheels and couldn't make it up the stage steps. Organizers had to pause the contest for fifteen minutes while she rebuilt her costume on stage. It was a great success, however, and the crowd went crazy when she was assembled.

BIG APPLE CON COSTUME CONTEST[11]

Event: Big Apple Convention
http://www.nycbm.com/
Date: 2014
How Many Participants: 20–35

The Big Apple Comic Con is a one-day comic book convention in New York City that was started by Mike Carbo in 1996. It focuses primarily on comic books versus other fandoms and features many artists, comic book professionals, and a costume contest hosted by Captain Zorikh Lequidre. Captain Zorikh organizes such contests for a variety of events and manages to run them successfully without any cost to the event or himself. He approaches local stores and artists to sponsor the prizes and offers sponsorships for the posters marketing the event to businesses such as local costume shops. His advice to libraries is to find a business or individual who wants to support them and also reach the same audience that will be present at the contest.

Zorikh uses his own organizational method for running the costume contest, which he refers to as "seat of your pants" style. He has each participant come up on stage one by one as he hands them the microphone. They each have one minute to say who their character is and to do something that their character would do. Afterward he has everyone line up on stage, and participants are judged by the "applause-o-meter" system in which the audience decides who has the best costume and/or character. He places all of the prizes on a table on the side, and winners, starting with the most popular, can choose their own prizes. He always tries to make sure that everyone gets a prize so that everyone feels good leaving the contest. He suggests that cosplay contest hosts can also be creative and segment the group into smaller sections based on fandoms. Prizes can then be awarded to the best superhero costume or the best *Star Wars* cosplay, and so on. The benefits to his audience-judging style are that it makes the event seem less serious and more fun, and also there is no time needed for everyone to wait while the judges confer about the winners. Additionally, this is a very low-tech way of approaching a cosplay contest because all that is needed is a single microphone for the host which can be shared with the contestants as they join him or her on stage.

NOTES

1. Case study based on an interview with Chad Mairn, information services librarian and Innovation Lab manager at St. Petersburg College, conducted by the author, January 20, 2015.

2. Case study based on an interview with Heather Warren Smith, youth services librarian at ELANCO Library, conducted by the author, January 27, 2015.

3. Case study based on an interview with Carrie Rogers-Whitehead, senior librarian of teen services at the Salt Lake County Library, conducted by the author, January 26, 2015.

4. Case study based on an interview with Kathleen Gruver, young adult librarian at the Burlington County Library System, conducted by the author, February 2, 2015.

5. Case study based on an interview with Sarah Hodge-Wetherbe, library associate at the Springfield City Library, conducted by the author, February 5, 2015.

6. Case study based on an interview with Kareemah Hamdan, branch manager; James Hudson, branch manager; and Kate Denwiddie, library specialist, all with the Chesterfield Public Library, conducted by the author, February 10, 2015.

7. Case study based on an interview with Rachelle Martin, youth services associate at the Raymond Timberland Library, conducted by the author, February 3, 2015.

8. Case study based on an interview with Carrie Rogers-Whitehead, senior librarian of teen services at the Salt Lake County Library, conducted by the author, January 26, 2015.

9. Case study based on an interview with Martha Buehler, youth services librarian at the Forest Park Public Library, conducted by the author, February 6, 2015.

10. Case study based on an interview with Brian Stephenson, brand marketing director; Justin Flores, content and talent coordinator; and Chris Malico, international content coordinator, all with ReedPop, conducted by the author, January 30, 2015.

11. Case study based on an interview with by Captain Zorikh Lequidre, cosplay contest host, conducted by the author, February 19, 2015.

6

Cosplay Programming for Libraries

Now that we've taken a look at the many ways that libraries are bringing cosplay-related programming into their communities, let's discuss exactly what it takes to organize events such as these. This chapter will provide instructions for how to run twelve different types of cosplay events in your library so that you can get started planning your own programs today.

PROJECT 1: HOST A COMIC OR ANIME CON IN YOUR LIBRARY!

Few events inspire and encourage cosplay like a comic or anime convention. A comic con is a one-day or multiple-day event filled with fun programming such as celebrity guest appearances; panels discussing comic art, video games, and science fiction and fantasy TV or films; sessions discussing specific fandoms such as *Harry Potter*, *Doctor Who*, *Buffy the Vampire Slayer*, or *Star Trek*, as well as workshops that teach attendees how to draw comics or design a board game, cosplay contests and photo shoots, and an exhibitor floor filled with pop culture vendors and artists offering eager con-goers everything from books and artist prints to figures and other collectibles. Anime cons follow the same basic formula; however, the programming and cosplay focus is based on anime and manga, and the exhibitor floor features vendors selling Japanese soda and candy, as well as anime-based collectibles, cosplay supplies, and Japanese clothing.

Both academic and public libraries have realized that hosting these types of events is a great way to bring in new readers, promote graphic novel and comics collections, and inform the community about anime, video game, and comics clubs at the library, as well as related upcoming workshops and events. Many libraries have already hosted their own comic and anime cons, and many more are planning them now. A one-day pop culture event such as this is an excellent vehicle to build relationships between the library and local businesses, artists, authors, and publishers. And it is a fantastic way to foster and support cosplay!

If you're ready to get started organizing your own comic or anime con for your library, this project will walk you through what's involved with planning and hosting one of these exciting events featuring fun and engaging programming with a literary bent. **Note:** Much of this project was informed by an interview and follow-up correspondence with Chad Mairn, information services librarian and Innovation Lab manager at St. Petersburg College and organizer of the Mid-Pinellas Comic and Maker Con, who was extremely generous with his time, as well as interviews with many other helpful librarians who are mentioned in the previous chapter.[1]

Costs and Funding

The first thing you'll want to think about is what types of costs will be involved and where you'll find funding for the event. Since you'll be hosting the event at the library, the largest cost involved with these events—the space—will already be taken care of. However, there are other costs involved, so as you plan and read through each section of this project, you will want to start to put together a budget for your anticipated expenses, depending on what exactly you're planning. Within each section, I will note the costs and make suggestions on the funding for the miscellaneous costs you might incur. But I would like to emphasize that it is completely possible to host an outrageously successful event on a shoestring budget of $500–$1,000. See the previous chapter for case studies that pinpoint the total cost for previous library comic cons. Below are some possible funding sources for your event.

Funding Sources

- The Friends of the Library group
- Local businesses that make donations or provide merchandise or tickets for prizes/giveaways
- Local colleges and universities
- Vendor/exhibitor fees for event participation
- The library's programming budget

Food Vendors

If you will be hosting an all-day event, it is highly recommended that you provide some sort of food and drink for attendees. Cosplayers, as well as many con-goers, tend to show up early and stay until the very end of the event, so you will want to avoid having costumed characters passing out on your library floor from hunger or dehydration. The easiest way to provide sustenance is to invite food trucks to come and set up in the library parking lot for the duration of the event. You can find listings of food trucks on Roaming Hunger (http://roaminghunger.com), a food truck rental directory that allows you to search vendors by location or cuisine type. Although you will not want to pay for a rental or full catering, you can use this directory to locate the trucks you'd like to invite and offer them the opportunity to set up during the event. You can also search for your local food truck association on the National Food Truck Association website (http://www.nationalfoodtrucks.org), which will provide listings of local food trucks. While booking food trucks for your event, you'll want to make sure that they each have a certificate of insurance, including worker's compensation and commercial auto liability, and have a current inspection permit and a license to serve food.

Special Guests

Give con-goers the unique opportunity to meet authors and artists by arranging some guest appearances. Comic book and manga artists, graphic novel authors, and even actors can make appearances, sign their work, and meet their fans. Start by looking locally; you may have these professionals in your area. Partner with local comic book shops, which will most likely be knowledgeable about where and how to find these guests. You will find that most comics shops will almost certainly be more than happy to help with this and will be eager to take part in your event as a vendor as well. You can locate your local comic book stores by going to http://www.comicshoplocator.com or calling 1-888-Comic-Book.[2]

Although many artists, authors, and special guests may offer to make an appearance gratis, you may need to offer a small honorarium for some guests, so you'll want to be prepared and have some funds on hand for this expense. You will most likely want to set up artists and other special guests at their own booths or tables where they can sit comfortably to meet fans and do signings. You can decide on the hours in which they will make an appearance and whether or not they will take part in any panels during their time at the con. This should all be agreed upon before the event, and an agreement should be signed. You will want to let them know ahead of time where they will be located so that they are prepared when they arrive.

Exhibitors/Vendors

Exhibitors and vendors are a large part of convention events as they provide attendees with news and information about their favorite books, films, and video game franchises, as well as having all manner of related merchandise for sale. Before inviting vendors to set up at your event, be sure to check that your library rules permit commercial activity on library grounds. Although most libraries are nonprofit organizations, they are most often allowed to host events where vendors can sell their own wares. They are oftentimes even allowed to charge those vendors a fee to participate, which may be one way to deflect some of the costs incurred by the event.

Not all exhibitors will be selling merchandise; some will simply be providing information about their group or organization. Local cosplay groups are oftentimes exhibitors at these events. Check Facebook and Meetup.com for local groups such as these. The library will also want to have an information booth or table set up with news and information about upcoming library events and easy registration for new library cards. Your local comic book shops will most likely have suggestions for how to spread the word about your event to potential vendors. Here are some examples of potential exhibitors and vendors:

- Comic book shops
- Comic book and graphic novel publishers
- Video game stores
- Gaming/hobby shops
- Craft and fabric stores
- Costume shops
- Local Etsy artists/store owners
- Other local conventions and events such as Renaissance fairs
- Arcades
- Local comics, cosplay, and gaming groups (Facebook and Meetup.com)
- Theme parks[3]

Once you start booking exhibitors, have them each sign an agreement to abide by the rules of the library during the event and assign them to a particular table or room so that they know where to go upon arrival. Also let exhibitors know when they can arrive in order to start setting up. If you will allow people to show up two hours before the event, you will need to be sure you have staff available on site when they arrive.

Featured Cosplayers

Featured cosplayers are well-regarded costumers or costumed performance groups who make appearances at conventions and special events. One example is the 501st Legion (http://www.501st.com), which is a fan-based, volunteer organization of costumers who create high-quality *Star Wars* costumes and wear them to events. They are well known for making charity event appearances. Imagine seeing Darth Vader, a contingent of Stormtroopers, and R2-D2 walk (or roll!) through the door of your library! The 501st Legion is an international organization with units around the world, so chances are there will be a unit near your library if you'd like to book them. Check their website for the event request form. Local cosplayer fan groups can often be found for *Ghostbusters*, *Star Trek*, *Firefly* (Browncoats), superheroes, and so on. Individual featured cosplayers can be found by looking to your local cosplay community; see chapter 3, "Places to Go, People to See," for tips.

Most featured cosplayers will expect to have a table where they can meet fans, take photos with fans, and sell their signed photos and other merchandise. If there is a performance aspect of their appearance or if they will be expected to serve as a judge in your cosplay contests, you will want to let them know ahead of time. It is also a standard practice to dedicate a private "green room" or changing area for featured cosplayers, as most won't come dressed in full costume. While most of these guests will make themselves available for free, there may be a fee for some performance groups or well-known cosplayers such as Yaya Han or Jessica Nigri.

Panels and Activities

Every comic book and anime convention is chock full of informational panels and fun activities, and this is an opportunity for the library to really shine. Librarians are well versed in organizing these types of events, such as instructional workshops, author talks and panels, gaming events, and so on. Here are just some of the events and activities that you may want to program into your library's convention.

Panels

These informative discussion sessions may be made up of fans, artists, authors, or celebrities. They can be organized by the library or by the library's anime or comic book clubs or by local cosplay organizations. Depending on the interests of your community and the guests that you have planned, the easiest way to schedule and come up with ideas for panels is to ask your patrons. You may have set up a planning Facebook group for the event; now is the time to use it. Put out a call for ideas regarding what types of panels patrons and attendees want to see. Below are just a few ideas:

- The art of Marvel Comics
- The history of DC Comics villains
- The films of Hayao Miyazaki
- The Whedonverse

- *Doctor Who* costumers
- Upcoming comics-based movies
- Comic artists spotlight
- *Attack on Titan*
- Cosplay and armor making
- Careers in comics

If there will be any PowerPoint or other presentations during your panels, be sure to let panelists know beforehand whether you'll be using a Windows or Mac computer. And make sure you have enough microphones for the panelists as well as for questions from the audience.

Classes and Workshops

Just like planning for the panels, your patrons will probably have a lot of input into what types of workshops they'd like to attend. Check in with your anime and comics clubs in your library and all the other branches in your library system; they may not only have suggestions but also recommendations of volunteers who can teach the workshops. Alternatively, you can approach your comic artist guests to see if they'd be interested in teaching a workshop. And finally, you may also want to check in with the local comic book shop, as they may themselves be able to teach a workshop or be able to suggest someone who can. Here are some ideas for workshops that other libraries have hosted:

- How to draw robots
- How to create a comic strip
- How to create your own villain
- How to draw chibi characters
- Manga drawing
- How to grade comics

Gaming

Oftentimes there are gaming rooms or separate areas at these events where con-goers can challenge each other and themselves in video games, board games, and card games such as *Magic the Gathering* and *Yu-Gi-Oh*. Check in with your gaming club as well as local gaming stores, as they may be willing to organize and run a tournament and even provide prizes for the winners. If you will be hosting a video game tournament, you may also consider projecting gameplay on large screens in other areas of the event beyond the video game room so that all of the attendees can watch, even if they are not participating in the tournament.

Movie Screenings

You may want to offer movie screenings as a part of your event. You can choose to have films playing in the background of some rooms or schedule a specific time that a movie will be shown, similar to the panel events. You will want to be sure to be copyright compliant by purchasing a public performance license for whatever films you'll be showing at your event. You can purchase a single-event license for about $110 or an annual, blanket license to show unlimited films in your library from Movie Licensing USA (http://library.movlic.com), a company that provides public performance site licenses to K–12 schools and public libraries. They offer licenses for popular Hollywood films and new releases, as well as anime films.[4]

Kids Crafts

Will there be children at your event? Most likely there will be. So why not set up a craft room with activities for them to take part in too? Past library comic con events have featured anime art drawing contests as well as steampunk jewelry creation. Other libraries have not only organized crafts for kids but also arranged volunteers to do face painting at the event.

Cosplay Contests

The cosplay contest is, for many, the most anticipated part of a comic or anime convention. It is the costumer's opportunity to showcase their hard work and creativity. And it is also a huge social event in which all attending cosplayers are gathered in one space and can meet and make new friends. The second project in this chapter goes into detail about what's involved with hosting a cosplay contest; however, in a nutshell, cosplayers present themselves and their costumes, they are judged, and the winners receive prizes. The cosplay contest is a great opportunity for you to seek sponsors to cover the costs of the prizes awarded. You can ask vendors to donate prizes such as tickets to events or merchandise to be given as prizes, and/or you can charge vendors a fee for their participation in the convention in order to cover the costs of purchasing prizes. Since this is such a big event within the con, you may want to schedule the cosplay contest toward the end of the day so that you can guarantee that people will stay for the duration of your event.

Other Suggested Activities

- Anime art contests
- Karaoke lounges[5]
- Live music/bands

Cosplay and Photography

Both cosplayers and photographers will want to take many photos at the event. You can encourage these photo shoots yet have them take place away from heavily trafficked areas of the con by setting up a photo booth area and/or scheduling a formal cosplay photo shoot.

Photo Booths and Backdrops

Since cosplay will likely be a large part of your event, you may consider designing a custom photo backdrop with the logo of the library and/or event for people (cosplayers as well as noncostumed attendees) to stand in front of and have their pictures taken, much as you'd see at a red carpet event. These are fairly standard at conventions and cosplay parties. This would be an added expense ranging from $100 to $300; however, you could approach a local printer that provides these and ask if they would donate the backdrop to the library or offer a discounted rate. You might also approach your Friends of the Library group, if you have one, and ask them to sponsor the backdrop. If you are at a larger institution, you might have a printing department that can create this type of thing for you. You may also consider providing a few superhero- or anime-themed props, such as Captain America's shield, Thor's hammer, or a Pikachu hat, so that noncosplayers can join in the fun with their photos.

Haco Stadium Tokyo.One is Japan's first cosplay theme park, which opened recently in Chiba, Japan. The park is made up of individual themed studio backgrounds that cosplayers can use for photo shoots, including both a classroom and a library studio,[6] both of which you likely have on site at your library. Why not challenge your cosplay or anime club to design an area for a cosplay photo studio for your event?

And if you're looking for something more awe inspiring and you have a larger budget, you could always rent a *Doctor Who* TARDIS photo booth that is sure to inspire plenty of photo shoots and selfies.

Cosplay Photo Shoots

At most major comic cons and anime events, there are scheduled cosplay photo shoots that are announced and placed on the formal schedule of events. For smaller cons, they consist of one large cosplay shoot in which everyone in costume meets at a particular place, such as on the front steps of the library, in order to have their photo taken with the whole group. At larger events, these can be divided into individual shoots according to fandom. For example, at DragonCon, there is a Marvel cosplay photo shoot scheduled each year in which cosplayers wearing a costume from the Marvel universe are welcome to join the group to have their photo taken. (See figure 19 for a photo of the event.) Other themed cosplay photo shoots at events might be *Homestuck*, *Adventure Time*, DC Universe, *Doctor Who*, *Star Wars*, *Star Trek*, *Skyrim*, and so forth.

These large photo shoots tend to get everyone involved either as a cosplayer or as a photographer. Con-goers who aren't wearing costumes are drawn to the event and want to take photos of the large group. This is an incredibly exciting and social experience for cosplayers, and for some, it is the highlight of the event. There will be cosplayers who are too shy to enter the cosplay contest but will still have the chance to experience the group camaraderie of the giant photo shoot. Group photos of all of the cosplayers at an event are great promotions for future events since photos from the shoot appear for weeks afterward on Facebook and social media as different people upload their photos.

Security and Fire Planning

It is highly recommended that you let your local sheriff or police department and your fire department know about your plans to host a comic con, even if you expect it to be small. Chad Mairn organized and hosted the first Seminole Library Mid-Pinellas Comic Con at which he hoped to attract a crowd of four hundred to six hundred people based on the attendance of a nearby library con. The event drew 3,500 people! These organizations will work with you in order to make sure your building is up to current fire code standards. They will discuss parking with you and also have EMTs standing by on the day of the event. If you have a campus security or library security department, you'll want to involve them in the planning stages of the event as well so that they can offer guidance and support.

Weapons Policy

You will want to develop a weapons policy for your event, and the reason is that a great majority of cosplayers' costumes are accompanied by props and weapons that they oftentimes make themselves. You will want to post this policy on your website ahead of time as cosplay-ers *do* look for this information before events in order to determine what they are allowed to bring. Keep in mind that oftentimes cosplayers do not have their own cars but are dropped off or take public transportation to these events, so they will have nowhere to put their weapons or props if they get to the event and they aren't allowed in. You will want to have someone at the door monitoring weapons as they come into the event.

The next chapter on "Issues, Tips, and Tricks" goes into more detail about what is typically allowed and prohibited at comic con events. In short, functional or realistic-looking firearms, projectile weapons, or metal-bladed swords always make the prohibited list. Props and weap-ons made of foam or cardboard are most often allowed into these events.

Space Planning

Space planning is something that should be kept in mind from the very early planning stages of the event. Talk to your facilities staff as well as your information technology (IT) department and ask them for recommendations. You'll want to ask questions such as

- How many exhibitors can we accept based on the space available?
- Will we need to rent tables and chairs for the exhibitors and vendors or do we have enough in the library?
- Where will we host panels and talks?
- Where will we host video game tournaments?
- Do we have or want a projector that will display the video game tournament on the library's large-screen TV?
- Where will we hold the cosplay contest?
- Do we have microphones for the cosplay contest?
- Are there nearby electricity outlets for the necessary microphones, gaming systems, com-puters, and so on?
- How large of a crowd are we expecting? Will we be having outdoor food trucks serving food and drinks to attendees? Let's think about how many restrooms we have available compared to the number of people we expect may come to the event. Portable toilets can be rented for a low cost, ranging from about $150 for four, depending on the vendor.

Once you have decided where you will have your exhibitors, guests, and vendors set up, you'll want to measure and plan out how many tables and chairs will fit in that space or spaces, if you are using more than one room. You can sketch this out by using a diagramming software program such as Microsoft Visio, or you can do it the old-fashioned way—walking around with a measuring tape and determining how many tables will fit in your vendor area. While you're planning such things, keep traffic patterns in mind. Where will people naturally walk in order to get from the panels to the vendor area to the craft room and to the restrooms? You don't want to set up obstacles for your con-goers. One of the most frustrating smaller cons that I've ever attended set up their vendor tables in a way that necessitated that attendees avoid large, floor-to-ceiling pillars every few feet while walking down the aisles, browsing mer-chandise. I had more than a few close misses as I was more interested in staring at the tables than watching where I was going. And finally, think about possible bottleneck areas and how you can avoid them or offer alternate paths. Even though you may only be expecting that five hundred people will attend your event, comic cons have become so popular in recent years that it would be wise to plan for many more attendees than estimated.

Library Signage

To keep traffic flowing well and to avoid confusion at the event, you'll want to design plenty of signage directing con-goers to the different areas that you have set up, as well as to provide clear labels for rooms and also for providing schedules outside of panel rooms.

Staff and Volunteers

Having plenty of library staff working the event is crucial to having a smoothly run convention. Since the event will most likely be held on a weekend, it may not be a day when all of the library staff are scheduled to work, so it is important to get everyone invested in the event from the very beginning. The more people who are involved with the planning, the more people will feel a sense of ownership of the event and will want to help out when the day arrives. It is also a very good idea to recruit nonlibrary staff volunteers who can help organize and oversee panels, craft activities, game rooms, and so on.

Staff and volunteers should be given badges or T-shirts clearly identifying them as convention crew so that attendees can easily spot them if they have questions about panels, locations, or anything else. Convention staff and crew will need to know the schedule of events and the locations of all panels, activities, guests, and exhibitors. It is a good idea to take everyone on a walkthrough of the library con setup the day before the event. Staff and volunteers should be encouraged to come to the event in costume in order to get into the spirit of the day.

Communication

You will want to arrange a way to communicate with all of the staff and planners involved in the event aside from e-mail. Set up a Dropbox folder or use Google Docs to share all of your strategy and planning documents with the team. This will keep communication flowing in an orderly and organized manner. You may also choose to use a Facebook group page to strategize months before the event. See further discussion on this topic in the next section. On the day of the event, you may want to use walkie-talkies or arrange to text with staff and volunteers who may be monitoring separate areas of the library, as well as with the fire marshal.

Marketing and Event Promotion

The most effective tool for event promotion according to all of the libraries I spoke with was Facebook. As a cosplayer and con-goer myself, I know that Facebook is the way that I receive the majority of my information about events such as these. I look for postings in the various groups that I belong to, such as Cosplayers & Photographers, New York Cosplayers Network, and so on. But you will want to cover your bases and use a combination of social and traditional media, as well as good old-fashioned word of mouth in order to promote your event. Below are some tips for spreading the word about your comic con.

Facebook

- Set up an event page for the event, which will run for the entire year up until the event, such as DragonCon 2017 or Animazement 2017. By setting up an event page including the date you allow people to RSVP so that you will get some idea of the amount of people interested in attending. It also lets people know the exact date and time of the event as well as directions.

- Create a planning group page for the event, such as AnimeNext 2017 Planning, and make it a closed group. Interested patrons can request and be approved to join the group. This page differs from the official event page in that those involved can post all of their brainstorming ideas that they have for organizing the event in private. You can also invite your teen clubs, such as comic book clubs, anime clubs, and gaming clubs, to join this group and give you feedback and suggestions for panels, guests, activities, and so on.
- Make a list of relevant cosplay, gaming, comics, and fandom Facebook groups for your area, such as Philadelphia Anime & Manga, North Texas Browncoats, North Carolina Retro Gamers, and so on. Join each of these groups and post a link to your Facebook event page.
- Make a list of all area comic cons and pop culture events. Contact these events and ask them to post a link to promote your library con on their pages. You will find that many of these events have followers in excess of one hundred thousand people![7]
- Use Facebook boosts to reach an audience of thousands for as little as $5 by boosting individual Facebook status updates and photos (such as your flyer!) about your event.
- Determine a daily budget and promote your event page by creating a Facebook ad by easily following the prompts on your event page.

Other Social Media

Be sure to post about your upcoming comic con on your library's blog and Twitter accounts for weeks leading up to the event. You will also want to post about it on your library website, and you may even want to have a dedicated website or set of pages for the event itself. This would be an excellent place to put online registration forms for vendors and participants in the cosplay contest.

Traditional Media

You will want to also use traditional forms of media to announce your event. Issue a press release and contact the following outlets and ask them to announce your event:

- Local TV news channels
- Local newspapers
- If you're an academic library, contact campus news; public libraries may have a library-wide newsletter
- Local visitor's bureau and chamber of commerce

Partnership Marketing

You don't have to go it alone; there are plenty of people and businesses that would be happy to spread the word about a fun, free, nonprofit event such as a library comic con.

- Arrange to have event flyers in other branches in your library system or across campus if you are an academic library.
- Ask vendors, exhibitors, and special guests to promote the event through their websites and social media outlets.

- Teen word-of-mouth cannot be underestimated; ask your teen groups to help spread the word to their friends.
- Participate in other local conventions and events by having an information table for the library and promote the event there.
- Partner with comic book shops, which have preexisting mailing lists and may offer to help promote the event if they are involved.

Event Programs

Event programs are important for letting attendees know what panels and activities you have planned for the day, their scheduled times, room locations, and so on, as well as information about guests and vendors. You will want to consider how many attendees you're expecting to have and then plan to print out an additional 10 percent, just to be safe. You can print these out yourself at the library or have an outside printer do it if you have extra funds or can arrange a donation from the printer. As an alternative to event programs, you can post a printed schedule in a central area of the con so that attendees will be aware of session times and locations. You will also want to post the schedule of events on your website in advance of the event so that con-goers are informed.

Copyright Concerns

Be cautious about using artwork on your flyers, programs, and promotional materials. You will want to have artists sign a release or permissions statement allowing you to use their artwork. You will also want to do your homework with regard to naming your con so that you don't run into infringement issues with your event name.

The Day-Before-the-Event Checklist

- Set up tables and chairs.
- Set up microphones and, if necessary, laptops and projectors for panels.
- Set up any movies to be played.
- Set up power cords, outlet strips, and cables.
- Test all audio, video, wi-fi, and other technology that you'll be using.
- Test the video games that will be played, especially if you are having a tournament.
- Set up the stage or area for the costume contest.
- Hang up signage directing people to different areas such as panels, extra seating areas, exhibitors, and so on.

After the Event

Keep up the momentum after the success of your convention by forming related comic book or anime clubs and providing information on your library's website and blog about pop culture–related collections and resources that the library offers, as well as upcoming events. Post photos of the event on Facebook and the library's website in order to get people interested in next year's event. In order to improve on what you did and start planning for your next event, survey con-goers to find out what worked and what didn't.

Library Comic Con Tips

- Make it free!
- Publish an advance program with the schedule so that people can plan which panels they want to attend.
- Post your weapons policy in advance so that cosplayers are aware of what they can bring with them.
- Post information about your cosplay contest in advance and allow online registration.
- Be sure to have plenty of signage on the day of the event.
- Allow vendors and food trucks to register in advance via an online form.
- Hold a contest to have your patrons design your event logo and/or flyers.
- Ask a local business to donate bags for con attendees to carry swag and purchases.

PROJECT 2: HOW TO HOST A COSPLAY CONTEST

An organized cosplay contest offers costumers the opportunity to highlight their creativity and all of the hard work that they put into fashioning their outfits. This event is often scheduled as one of the final activities of a comic con but can also be a part of a fandom club meeting, a library lock-in event, or a stand-alone occurrence. It is a time when cosplayers can gather together to show off their costumes to their peers as well as to an audience and have a chance to meet and speak with other cosplayers in the community. Although cosplay contests are competitive events, they are usually very good natured, and cosplayers often wish to participate for the sense of community alone. To this end, many cosplay contest organizers offer some sort of prizes for all of the participants so that everyone feels appreciated.

Coordinating a cosplay contest is a relatively low-budget and low-hassle event to plan as most libraries usually have some sort of audiovisual equipment on hand and little more is required beyond knowledge and planning. Here's a walkthrough of what's involved with planning one of these events for your library.

Event Promotion

The first thing that you will want to do is think about how to get the word out about your event. If this will be featured as a part of a larger event, such as a library comic con or club meeting, be sure to include at least an announcement such as "Cosplay Contest" on the flyers, event notices, Facebook event pages, and tweets. Take a look at some of the marketing and event promotion tips in the previous project and incorporate those. Additionally, you will want to provide links to the cosplay contest rules so that costumers will know how to prepare for what is and is not allowed, your weapon's policy (see the "Rules" section below for an example policy), and an online registration form.

Categories

Next, consider how you will organize your event and decide what the main structure will be. Most cosplay contests will specify that entrants represent a particular category or subgenre of fandom and pop culture, such as

- comic books
- movies
- TV
- anime
- video games
- literature
- science fiction

Participants in each category are then judged and compared to others in that same class. Other events may subdivide the contest by age ranges:

- Children ages five through twelve
- Adults ages eighteen and over (thirteen and over with parental permission)

And still others may segment their contests by skill level:

- Beginner
- Intermediate
- Advanced

Skits

Some cosplay contests allow contestants to perform brief (two to three minute) skits representing their character or characters if they are part of a cosplay group. Skits can consist of dancing, singing, acting out a particular scene, or any impression representative of the character portrayed. These are usually set to prerecorded music, and microphones are generally not allowed. Skits would involve more planning and logistics on the day of the show; however, it may make the contest more engaging for some participants, as well as for the audience. Most events that do allow skits do not necessitate that all entrants perform one. Bear in mind that allowing skits will lengthen the time of your contest.

Individuals and Groups

Contest organizers will want to make it clear whether or not they will allow both individual and group entries and whether they will be judged together or separately.

Costume Specifications

Most cosplay contests that take place at major comic cons specify that the prefabricated or store-bought costumes may not compete; however, most of the smaller cons and cosplay events do not make this distinction about handmade versus purchased costumes. Since this event will be held in the library, you will want to make it as inclusive as possible and will probably want to skip including too many rules pertaining to costumes. However, you will want to specify in the rules that certain materials are restricted, as are offensive costumes. See the example in the "Rules" section for more on this topic.

To Prejudge or Not to Prejudge?

If you want to get a little fancy with your event, you may consider an added round of prejudging. This involves contestants meeting with the panel of judges before they take the stage in order to describe their costumes in detail, including how they made them, what their inspiration was, and so forth. This round would work well for cosplay contests that are run by the cosplayers themselves or as a way to gather information for announcing contestants and explaining their costumes in a fashion show–style cosplay contest.

Rules

Every cosplay contest has a set of rules, even if they are very simple or are announced on the day of the contest, as may be the case for more informal events. These rules define the structure of your event and determine who may participate. Rules are often posted on an event website or Facebook page, and cosplayers do look for these guidelines when preparing their costumes. Here is a basic set of rules that would be appropriate for a library cosplay contest:

- All participants must fill out a liability waiver (adults) or have a signed parental permissions form (children) filled out before the start of the contest.
- All entrants must represent a character or component from one of the following pop culture categories: movies, television, anime, science fiction, comic books, video games, or literature.
- Group entries are (or are not) allowed.
- Original costumes not representing a particular character are (or are not) allowed.
- Skits are (or are not) allowed.
- Participants may enter only once and wear one costume. Participants may not enter as both an individual and a group member.
- Each participant's time on stage is limited to approximately one minute.
- Nudity or the illusion of nudity is not allowed. All costumes must be suitable for a family-friendly event.
- Profanity (including messages on clothing) is not allowed.
- Obscene or offensive costumes are not allowed.
- All prop weapons must adhere to the library's **weapons policy**, which is as follows:
  - Prop weapons that are made of light materials such as foam, cardboard, or wood are permissible. Prop firearms and other weapons must not be so realistic that they could be mistaken for actual weapons. Barrels of all prop firearms must have brightly colored caps in the barrels.
  - No functional firearms (including air soft guns, paintball guns, etc.) or realistic-looking firearms that might be confused with functional firearms.
  - No projectile weapons of any type, including water guns.
  - No metal-bladed weapons, including swords.
  - No real blunt weapons such as nunchaku or brass knuckles.
  - No hard prop weapons made of metal or fiberglass.
  - No fireworks or explosives.
- Violating any of these rules may result in being disqualified from the competition.
- HAVE FUN![8]

Judges

Judges for your contest will be easy to find. They can be cosplayers from the local community, sponsors who have donated prizes, or even librarians! A panel of three to four judges is preferable; however, I've been to more than a few cosplay contests that were judged simply by audience applause and the emcee's final decision. At larger events, such as New York Comic Con, judges are selected based on relevant background and experience, such as costume designers, famous cosplayers, celebrities, and so forth; however, a group of interested and engaged librarians and/or sponsors can be just as effective.

Prizes

There is plenty of wiggle room when it comes to prizes for cosplay contests. As I mentioned earlier, cosplayers are less interested in the prize at the end than they are with getting together with a group of like-minded pop culture costumers for an event such as this. With that being said, if your contest is a part of a larger event, such as a library comic con, there are many opportunities to be had by approaching vendors to donate prizes such as gift cards, tickets to local events, or media items from publishers such as books or DVDs. You may even want to specify that vendors must make a monetary donation toward the cosplay contest in order to participate in the library con. If you aren't able to acquire any prizes in these ways, get creative! Print out some cool certificates or take a look around the library for extra advance copies of books. Prizes can be awarded for a variety of titles:

- Best in Category (**Note:** if one or more of your categories has only a few entrants, feel free to combine categories!)
- Best in Show
- Best Young Cosplayer
- Best Craftsmanship
- Most Creative
- Most Humorous[9]
- Many more; feel free to think up your own!

Registration and Permissions

Cut down on what you need to do on the day of the event by offering online preregistration. Think about the information that you will want to gather about the participant and his or her costume, including the character and category he or she is representing. Also, provide both the adult waiver form and the child permission form as links from the registration form. Have participants print out those forms to sign and bring with them to the event. You will also want to offer on-site registration the day of the event for those who just found out about the contest. Here's an example registration form:

- Name:
- Name of parent/guardian if under thirteen:
- Age:
- Your costume character (or group) name:
- Series/book/movie/game the character is from:

- Category:
- Any necessary additional information about your costume:

Backstage

Set up a backstage area, or, as the organizers for the New York Comic Con contest call it, a "cospitality lounge," that will serve as a kind of green room with mirrors and supplies such as simple sewing kits, glue, and tape, that may be needed for last-minute costume malfunctions. This can be dedicated or reserved restrooms as well as other areas of the library where cosplayers can prepare and primp before their stage debut.[10]

Stage Setup

Create an off-stage area where cosplayers can line up as they get ready to go on stage. This will keep a large crowd of cosplayers from forming in doorways, by the audience, and so on, but also will make their grand entrance an "ahhh" moment for the participants and the audience. The off-stage area could consist of a nearby stacks aisle or a place behind a room divider.[11]

Libraries will want to have a simple audiovisual system set up, consisting of one to two microphones for the emcee and judges panel, as well as speakers for announcing contestants and playing background music, which can be played from an iPhone or other device. These systems can be purchased at most music stores as well as from online websites such as Sweetwater.com or Musiciansfriend.com if the library doesn't already own such equipment.

The Event

At the time of the event, direct cosplayers to walk on stage and strike a pose or two while they are announced and then have them exit the stage area on the other side. If your library doesn't have a formal stage area, clear out an area that can be used as such. While you may not be equipped to live stream your event as some of the mega-cons do, you can certainly have someone taking video, which you can upload later to the library's Facebook page and YouTube channel.

Alternatives

Not all cosplayers want to take part in a competitive event such as this. Some are shy, while others just don't want to be judged. Still others may be too young. So you may want to think of activities that these cosplayers can take part in as well, aside from the contest. Here are few ideas:

- Host a cosplay parade following the contest that all cosplayers can participate in and enjoy as a group.
- Allow "walk-on only" entries for those who want to show off their costumes and have a walk on stage but do not want to participate in the judging component.
- Host a Hallway Cosplay Contest at which contestants can register and be evaluated by the panel of judges separate from the public cosplay contest.

PROJECT 3: HOW TO FORM A
COSPLAY CLUB IN YOUR LIBRARY

A great way to keep teens and other library patrons engaged with your library and its collection is by forming a cosplay club. Clubs and their events help to build community among your library patrons, bring new patrons into the library, and promote your collections. They are often a low-cost way to program as a single staff member can often helm monthly meetings and events, especially with the help of club leaders, and most of the expenses involved consist only of snacks. If your library has other teen clubs such as anime, book, or video game clubs, you can look to their structure for tips and guidance and also reach out to those members to see if there is enough interest to merit forming a cosplay club in your library. The following is a blueprint of what is involved with forming a library cosplay club.

Audience

Consider who you want to include in your cosplay club. Will this only be open to teens in the library? Or will it be open to everyone with an interest in cosplay? You will want to make the audience clear when promoting your club and creating your flyers and online pages. If the club is only for teens, you'll want to specify something along the lines of "for library patrons ages twelve through eighteen." If there is enough interest, you may consider creating both teen and adult cosplay clubs.

Communication and Promotion

How will you keep your cosplay club members and potential members (and parents!) informed? Communication is the key to the success of any club.[12] Let people know what your club is doing, watching, and planning in the future. This will keep members coming back and will help recruit new members. In sum, keep your group informed by promoting the club where people will see the announcements. You can promote your club and its activities on your library's website in the Teen or Youth Services Department section, which is great, but it is static and can only be used to inform patrons rather than gather feedback, RSVPs to future events, patron photos, and so on. I would also suggest that you create a Facebook page for the group, as many teens will find their information there. This is where you can create events for each upcoming meeting and event that the club is hosting, along with information about what to bring, what to wear, and so forth. Patrons can RSVP to events, letting librarians and their friends know that they'll be there, and in doing so, spread the word to their network of friends. Word of mouth is often the most effective form of promotion among teens. Tell club members (or if you're just starting, members of your other library clubs) to spread the word in school, and so on.[13]

Creating flyers to be posted in the library and at local businesses such as comic book stores, supermarkets, bookstores, and costume shops can also be very effective. And targeted placement of flyers or bookmarks promoting your cosplay club in all of your relevant collections, such as within books on costuming, comics, and manga, can be quite effective as well.[14] Librarians can make it a habit to replace these promotional materials as returns come in. You may also consider creating an e-mail mailing list for the group.

Logistics

When will your cosplay club meet? Most of these types of programs, such as book, anime, and gaming clubs, meet once per month for about one to two hours. You will want to decide what day and time works best for your meetings with library staff. But you will also want to bear in mind that your main audience may be teens, so you will want to factor in when they are most available. Next you'll want to determine where in the library the club will meet. Will your club be making items for their cosplays during meetings? If so, it may be optimal to have them meet in your makerspace. Alternatively, a meeting room with a large conference table would be great for crafting-focused groups. If your group will be watching comics movies or anime during their meetings, you will want to reserve an area with a large-screen TV and plenty of comfy seating.

Staffing

A single member of staff, most likely the youth services librarian, should be able to manage a cosplay club on their own; however, they may want to partner with the makerspace staff if the library has one. As the club grows, leaders may emerge within the group and be able to run monthly meetings and events on their own.

Food

During monthly meetings, most library clubs provide some free snacks, for example, chips, healthy snacks, Japanese munchies such as Pocky, or perhaps even pizza if it will be a long meeting. Some meetings may even incorporate snacks into the programming activities, such as making candy sushi or a chopstick Ramen-eating contest. Whatever the theme, it is important that some snacks are provided.

Icebreakers

Start things off with a way to break the ice such as a cosplay show-and-tell. If cosplayers have come to the meeting in costume, they can introduce themselves and explain their costumes. Alternatively, if they aren't in costume, they can discuss what they've cosplayed in the past and/or what they are interested in cosplaying. Games that can be played as icebreakers can include

- Name that comics or anime soundtrack song
- A comics trivia game that challenges players to guess the identity of the character whose picture is taped to their back
- Comics or anime jeopardy

Activities

What will your cosplay club "do" at monthly meetings? Not only will this type of club allow people that share a similar interest to socialize and meet new friends, it is also an opportunity to learn from each other. Club members can

- Brainstorm ideas for new costumes and props
- Share advice for how to make costumes
- Plan group cosplays with others in the club, for example, a *Harry Potter* cosplay group, an *X-Men* cosplay group, an *Attack on Titan* cosplay group
- Have cosplay workshops on armor building, sewing, wig styling, and so on
- Have sewing and craft days to work on projects together, share sewing machines, and so forth
- Have photo shoot days
- Bring in guest speakers
- Plan cosplay panels for the library's comic or anime con
- Plan group meet-ups at local conventions
- Have cosplay swaps in which teens who are bored with their current or past costumes can bring them to the club and swap them for other pieces, props, or full costumes
- Have cosplay contests and events
- Take part in cosplay challenges such as Cosplay Iron Chef (rules in appendix A)
- Host cosplay dances, library lock-ins, and other events
- Just have fun and watch movies, play video games, sing karaoke, draw, or craft

Viewings

You may want to show anime or film screenings to inspire cosplayers as a part of some of your meetings or events, but you will want to be sure to be copyright compliant by purchasing a public performance license for whatever you'll be showing. You can purchase a single-event license for about $110 or an annual, blanket license to show unlimited films and anime in your library from Movie Licensing USA (http://library.movlic.com), a company that provides public performance licenses to K–12 schools and public libraries. They offer licenses for popular Hollywood films and new releases, as well as anime films.

If you do decide to have screenings, pay close attention to ratings. If it's a teen cosplay club, be sure that the film or anime is rated G, PG-13, TV-PG, or TV-14. Also be sure to show a variety of movies and different anime series at your events; you can have members vote on what will be shown via Facebook polls before the event. In addition to DVDs, the library can stream both films and anime from apps and sites such as

- Netflix
- Hulu
- Amazon Prime
- Crunchyroll
- Funimation
- Viz[15]

Plugging the Library

During each meeting, you will want to set aside some time to plug the library and its relevant collections and events. You can either discuss your resources during a club break, perhaps interjecting with a joke such as "and now a message from our sponsors!" or you can bring a cart of related collections to the club for members to discover. Alternatively, you can have flyers sitting on the table(s) where the group will be meeting, promoting either a related event or collection. You can feature comics and manga collections that the library holds, as well as books and other resources on costume design, sewing, fashion, and cosplay itself.

Waivers and Permission Slips

In addition to keeping your membership and their parents in the know about what your group is doing and watching, you will want to think about the need for waivers and permission slips. These will inform parents that the content of the movie or anime you plan to show contains mild violence or other content that they'll need to know about and grant permission for members to take part in group photo shoot events, attend library lock-ins, or enter a library cosplay contest. In addition to informing parents about *exactly* what the club is doing, these forms and waivers protect the library in case there are any questions following the meetings or events. Think about whether or not you need to draft one of these permission slips or waivers before each of your meetings.[16]

Club Officers

As the club starts to take off, you may consider instituting a small board or committee that will lead the group, made up of officers such as president, vice president, secretary, treasurer, and so on. This will take some of the burden of group management off of the library staff and empower teens to be leaders among their peers. This also gives the teens a real sense of ownership and investment.[17]

Fund-Raising

While most of your cosplay club meetings will involve very little expenses beyond providing snacks, your club leaders may suggest organizing more ambitious activities, for example, workshops with professional instructors; special cosplay or comics/anime guests; materials to make their costumes, such as Worbla, craft foam, and so on; or even tools for making costumes, such as sewing machines. In that case, you will want to motivate your cosplay club to do some fund-raising in order to cover the expenses involved. For example, the club could host a maid (and butler) café in the library. This would be especially popular as a part of a library anime con in which they would serve *kawaii* (cute) food and drinks to café patrons while in costume. They could also create fandom-related crafts that they could sell to raise money, such as anime or comics felties and plushies. Alternatively they could host a good old-fashioned bake sale!

PROJECT 4: HOW TO HOST A COSPLAY PROPS 3-D PRINTING EVENT

Three-dimensional (3-D) printing has opened up a whole new world of possibilities for cosplayers, limited only by their imaginations. With these remarkable machines, motivated makers can bring to life whatever they can design using 3-D modeling software such as Tinkercad. From helmets and props to jewelry and costume pieces, the possibilities are endless. And this opens up a myriad of opportunities for libraries not only to serve as partners in the production process but to offer STEM (science, technology, engineering, and math) educational programming to makers of all ages. Skills learned through creating 3-D objects using computer-aided drafting (CAD) applications are transferable to real-world career paths in many fields.

Aside from its educational value, 3-D printing satisfies a desire to create something from nothing, to "make" an object of one's own and to make it exactly as imagined. This creative desire is what fuels many cosplayers, who are usually willing to learn whatever new techniques or skills are required in order to craft their costumes. I first discovered 3-D printing when I was working on a cosplay for Khan Noonien Singh (from *Star Trek: The Wrath of Khan*). I was confident about how to make all of the different costume elements with the exception of his necklace, which is made of metal and very distinctive in shape. I thought about shaping it using Worbla or even polymer clay; however, I knew that there must be a way to make it look more authentic and professional. I did a quick search for "Khan" on Thingiverse, and the very first result was an exact replica of his necklace. I realized then that I needed to figure out how to use 3-D printers and their accompanying software as they would substantially improve my costuming ability. (See figure 8 for a photo.)

Why not bring this realization to potential makers in your community by hosting a props-making event in your library? Janet Hollingsworth, teen guide and 3-D printing guru at Anythink Brighton in Brighton, Colorado—home of Anythink's first makerspace, the Studio at Anythink Brighton—shared her opinion that cosplay programming such as this would serve as "incredible bait to get teens and tweens to start learning computer-aided design." Janet facilitates many 3-D printing events in her library and finds that the most successful ones are those with a clear design objective. And they are also the ones that encourage collaboration among learners.[18]

Planning the Event

Be sure to market the event as a cosplay props-making event so that participants will come equipped with ideas about what they want to make during the session. Plan for a one-and-a-half-hour workshop in your computer lab. This type of programming will be appropriate for ages six to eight and older; however, you will want to have a generic library account set up for those participants under thirteen to share, as Tinkercad requires users to be over thirteen or else go through a strict parental-approval process. If you aren't confident in your 3-D modeling abilities, you may want to invite local maker volunteers or even 3-D printer representatives to attend your first couple of sessions.

Inspiration and Patterns

Before diving into the ins and outs of computer-aided design, it would be a good idea to get everyone excited about what kinds of things they can create by using such a program. A great place for this type of inspiration is Thingiverse (http://www.thingiverse.com). It is the largest 3-D printing community in the world with a collection of over one hundred thousand 3-D printable objects or patterns that are available for free download. On this website, you can browse the collection of printable "things" or search for areas of interest. This website is chock-full of inspiration for fledgling cosplay makers. For example, a search for the term "cosplay" brings back more than three hundred patterns, including:

- Star Lord's boot jets from *Guardians of the Galaxy*
- A *Spirited Away* face mask

- Tony Stark's Arc Reactor from *Iron Man*
- A full-scale wearable Stormtrooper helmet
- A Wonder Woman cosplay belt buckle
- Link's Deku Shield from *The Legend of Zelda: Ocarina of Time*

Additionally, searching specific fandoms is also very successful. For example, a search for "Doctor Who" brings back 120 patterns, including:

- A *Doctor Who* TARDIS model
- A Weeping Angel
- A Dalek
- A Sonic Screwdriver
- *Doctor Who*–themed Christmas ornaments

Other sources of free 3-D patterns include:

- https://sketchfab.com
- https://3dwarehouse.sketchup.com

Tinkercad

Tinkercad (https://www.tinkercad.com) is one of the most accessible, easy-to-use 3-D modeling software programs available today and has had over four million designs created with it. Tinkercad is particularly useful for libraries as it is free and completely web-based, so no software installation is necessary. This application enables makers to create 3-D designs from scratch using a variety of helpful shapes and tools; it also allows makers to import and edit existing 3-D files found on websites such as Thingiverse.

For this event, you will want to walk participants through the following features of the Tinkercad program and then give them a brief demo on how to create a 3-D object before letting them "tinker" on their own and in groups. An alternative to creating a 3-D object from scratch might be to download a Thingiverse file and edit it using Tinkercad.

Account Setup

Everyone will need to set up an account with their own e-mail addresses or else log in with the library's generic account. The sign-up process is very brief.

The Interface and Tools

The Tinkercad interface consists of a central workplane on which shapes are manipulated, view and perspective tools on the left side, and shapes on the right side that can be dragged onto the workplane. Shapes include seventeen geometric shapes such as boxes and cylinders, letters of the alphabet, numbers, symbols, and a few extras, all of which can be placed on the workplane either as solid shapes or negative ones, which are holes. Additional workplanes can also be added from this toolbar and attached to any surface of any shape in order to build on it. Each pane on the workplane space measures one millimeter and the snap grid, or size that a shape will automatically snap to, is set at one millimeter by default; however, this can be easily adjusted on the bottom right of the central design pane.

Navigating the Workspace

The easiest way to navigate around the workplane and shapes is by using the mouse. Holding down the right mouse button anywhere in the central design pane will allow you to shift perspectives and orientation with regard to the shapes and the workplane. Scrolling the mouse button forward or back controls zooming in and out of the central pane. Alternatively, you can also use the view tools on the left-hand side of the interface.

Manipulating Shapes

Working with shapes of all types is easy in Tinkercad. Simply choose a geometric shape, such as a box, from the tools on the right and drag it onto the workplane. Adjust the size of the shape by manipulating the white box handles surrounding the shape. Similar to editing a 2-D image, grabbing the corner handles adjusts both the width and height of the object at the same time, while grabbing just a top handle makes the image taller or shorter while keeping the width the same. The added variable with 3-D objects is that you also have the ability to adjust the depth of the shape. Once you have a shape on the workplane, an "Inspector" dialog box pops up with choices of color, as well as the option to make the shape a hole rather than a solid.

Building 3-D Objects

Creating 3-D objects is quite simple using Tinkercad, although it does take some patience to build complex ones. There are a few concepts that you will want to acclimate yourself to in order to start thinking in a three-dimensional manner.

Groups: Hold down shift and select multiple shapes that you want to group together as one and select "Group" on the top of the central design pane. These groups of shapes can then be moved and resized together.

Workplanes: Workplanes can be placed on the top, side, or on any surface of a shape in order to place other shapes on top of the original one. Once you're done, select "Workplane" again from the right toolbar and place the workplane on the bottom in order to return to the original view.

Holes: Holes can be created out of any shape and then placed inside of, on the corner of, or anywhere on any shape in order to create negative space in that shape. But in order to get the shape to create a hole, you must group it with the solid shape that it is attached to.

How to Build a House

To demonstrate this, let's build a simple house by dragging a box shape onto the workplane. Next drag a triangular roof shape into the central pane. But how do you get the roof onto the top of the box shape? Here you have two choices: you can manipulate the black cone-shaped handle near the top of the roof shape and try and get it to the same height as the box shape, or an easier option is to place a workplane on the top surface of the box and drag a roof shape onto it. Next, reselect "Workplane" from the right and click on the bottom of the central design pane in order to go back to the original view. Press and hold shift and select the two shapes and group them. You can also create a door and doorknob in the same manner. Finally, let's create a chimney from the hexagonal prism shape. Resize it and place it on the roof. Before going back to the original view, make a copy of the shape by selecting it and pressing CTRL + C. Press CTRL + V to paste the shape. Adjust this second chimney so that it is slightly smaller than the original and place it over or inside of the other one, but instead of making it a solid shape, make it a hole, so that it is the hollow part of the chimney. Now go back to the original view and select both chimneys—the solid and the hole inside of it—and select "Group." You will now see that the program subtracts the negative shape, or the hole, from the solid chimney.

How to Build a TARDIS

You can demonstrate how to build complex shapes by using the above house demonstration, or you can get fancy and show participants how they can build a TARDIS using Tinkercad. There are several example TARDIS shapes available to start with in the gallery. You can search for one to start with and show students how they can edit it, or you can start from scratch. If you're not sure what a TARDIS looks like, or if you just want to have concept art on hand, simply Google the term "TARDIS" and many images of the *Doctor Who* time machine will return in the results. A basic TARDIS can be built by using simple shapes without much modification. Here are some dimensions and instructions. Measurements are given in width $\times$ height $\times$ depth.

1. Create the TARDIS base with a blue box adjusted to these dimensions: 24 mm $\times$ 24 mm $\times$ 2 mm.
2. Create a blue box measuring 20 mm $\times$ 20 mm $\times$ 38 mm, which will be placed on top of the base.
3. On each side, create eight 1 mm indentations in each of the sides of the police box by creating holes made from boxes that are 6 mm $\times$ 6 mm each and 1 mm deep. To start, attach a new workplane to one of the sides. Create the first 6 mm $\times$ 6 mm $\times$ 1 mm box and position it on the grid. Use the black cone handle and push it just 1 mm inside of the blue box. Change it to a hole. Now copy and paste it using CTRL + C and then CTRL + V. Use the arrow keys to move the next box into position on that same side. Repeat until you have all eight boxes in position. Go back to the main view, select all of the small holes and the box, and group them.
4. Create a black box shape that measures 24 mm $\times$ 2.25 mm $\times$ 24 mm and place it on top of the blue box.
5. Create a smaller blue box measuring 2 mm $\times$ 20 mm $\times$ 20 mm and place it on top of the black one.
6. Create a blue pyramid that measures 2 mm $\times$ 18 mm $\times$ 18 mm.
7. To top it off, create a white cylinder that measures 3 mm $\times$ 3 mm $\times$ 6mm. Instead of trying to balance it on top of the pyramid, place a workplane on the black box and center the cylinder on it so that it comes up out of the pyramid.
8. Top off your TARDIS with a blue cone measuring 4 mm $\times$ 4 mm $\times$ 1mm. To get it to center, you may want to change the snap grid measurement to 0.5 mm.
9. Congratulations! You've created a 3-D model of a TARDIS!

While this should be enough to intrigue participants, you can optionally

a. Add text to the black box that says "Police Public Call Box" and/or
b. Add white window cut outs to the top two indentation squares using the same process as in step 3 but instead adding white colored boxes and subtracting others.

Download for 3-D Printing

When you've got your 3-D object in the shape that you want it, select the Design menu and choose "Download for 3D Printing." Depending on your 3-D printer, choose the file type to save your object in. The .stl file type is the most common. You are now ready to send this file to the 3-D printer.

Beginner Lessons

Tinkercad provides many beginner tutorial lessons. You may want to suggest that participants pair up and walk through all of the four to six lessons before they attempt to create their own designs. This will get them familiar with the tools and interface.

One-on-One Sessions

You can let students create their own 3-D objects while you are on hand to provide assistance. Near the end of the session, when participants have completed their designs, you have the opportunity to sit with them and discuss the strengths of their design as well as any voids or errors that may occur during printing due to disconnected shapes, and so on.[19]

The Print Queue

Printing a 3-D object takes time, sometimes up to forty-five minutes to an hour in order to print out a small design, depending on the level of detail. Therefore, you can allow each participant to send their designs to the printer when they are done and come back at another time to pick up their object.[20]

Other 3-D Modeling Software

In case you want to explore beyond Tinkercad, here are some other tools and applications.

- Autodesk 123D Design (http://www.123app.com)
- Sketchup (http://sketchup.google.com/intl/en/download)
- Blender (http://www.blender.org/)
- 3D Tin (http://www.shapeways.com/creator/tools/)
- Inkscape (https://inkscape.org/en/)
- Makerbot Desktop (http://makerbot.com/desktop)
- Cura (http://wiki.ultimaker.com/Cura). This program prepares 3-D files for printing, checking for "manifold errors" such as gaps in the 3-D model or surfaces of the object that don't connect to each other.

Encouraging 3-D Culture in Your Library

Janet Hollingsworth of Anythink Brighton stresses how important it is to build enthusiasm and gain staff buy-in and support for 3-D printing. It can be a frustrating program to support since today's 1.0 3-D printers often break down and need troubleshooting. However, Janet turns those breakdowns into teachable moments with workshop participants who are fascinated to see the printer opened up and repaired. Although she is an engineer by trade, she suggests that libraries can enlist an adept technician or volunteer to assist with these programs. Jackie Kuusinen, branch manager/experience expert at Anythink Brighton, stresses that the 3-D printer is simply the tool that they employ in order to teach valuable skills and make their community members more viable in the workforce. She sums up what it means to take part in one of these maker events quite well when she says, "It's not what they do in the studio, it's who they become as a result."[21]

PROJECT 5: HOW TO HOST A CREATE-YOUR-OWN ARMOR WITH WORBLA EVENT

Hosting an armor-building event in your library is a sure way to attract cosplayers and perhaps even a few noncostumers who are curious about how they too can design and create their own armor items. This type of program will teach participants how to create their own patterns and armor, but it also may be the only chance that some participants will have to work with a thermoplastic such as Worbla since it is out of the price range of many cosplayers. Armor building can be organized as a single event or as a workshop series teaching not only armor creation but techniques of painting and weathering armor, as well as the many ways to attach armor to the body with straps, D-rings, hook-and-loop fasteners such as Velcro, and so on.

Materials Needed

- Plastic wrap
- Masking tape
- Permanent marker
- Scissors
- Worbla
- Craft foam sheets
- Hot air gun
- Gloves to protect from heat
- Spray primer
- 80 or 150 grit sandpaper
- Black spray paint
- Gold, silver, copper metallic spray paints
- Acrylic paints, various colors
- Paint brushes, various sizes

Age Restrictions

Since this workshop event will involve using a hot air gun as well as a heated thermoplastic material, you will likely want to restrict participants to ages twelve and up since participants must be responsible and aware of the dangers of using power tools as well as working with hot materials.

Facilities

It goes without saying that this type of programming works best in libraries that are equipped with makerspaces. However, that being said, there are many cosplayers, myself in-

Figure 1. Cosplayers featured in TLC's *Cake Boss* TV show for the Amazing Spider-Man fiftieth-anniversary season finale episode. *Photo by Ron Gejon Photography*

Figure 2. Kamui Cosplay in Daedric armor inspired by the video game *Skyrim*. Armor and weapons made with Worbla (see chapter 6, project 5 to find out how). *Copyright 2015 by* Kamui cosplay.com

Figure 3. Casual Dredd Cosplay by Dadpool Cosplay and Props. Body armor made with EVA foam, helmet made with cardboard (see chapter 6, project 8 to find out how).

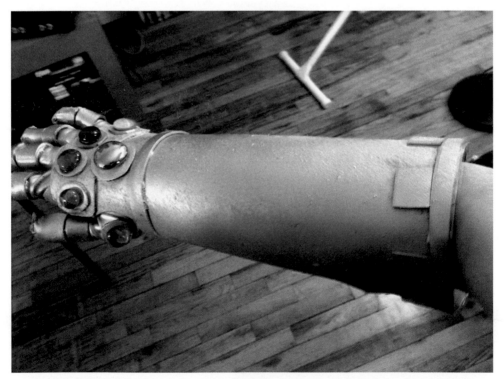

Figure 4. Infinity Gauntlet made with craft foam (see chapter 6, project 7 to find out how).

Figure 5. Zod in Kryptonian battle armor from *Man of Steel* by Striking Cosplay. Armor made with Pepakura (paper) (see chapter 2 for more). *Photo by Cyberhead Designs*

Figure 6. West World Gnomon Chase Cosplay by Ed Crandell. Armor made with Pepakura (paper) (see chapter 2 for more). *Photo by Rachael Hill*

Figure 7. Giallo Girl as Gozer from *Ghostbusters* with a papier-mâché "Terror Dog" (see chapter 6, project 9 to find out how). *Photo by Ron Gejon Photography*

Figure 8. A 3-D printed replica of Khan's necklace inspired by *Star Trek II: The Wrath of Khan* (see chapter 6, project 4 to find out how).

Figure 9. DC Cosplayers East group photo shoot. *Photo by Carlos A. Smith Photography*

Figure 10. Greek Mythology at DragonCon Cosplay Group 2014. *Photo by Lionel Lum*

Figure 11. The Real Tampa Bay Ghostbusters (see chapter 4 for more).

Figure 12. An ELANCO Library After Hours Teen Fandom Event (see chapter 5 for more).

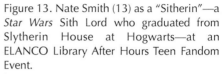

Figure 13. Nate Smith (13) as a "Sitherin"—a *Star Wars* Sith Lord who graduated from Slytherin House at Hogwarts—at an ELANCO Library After Hours Teen Fandom Event.

Figure 14. An ELANCO Library After Hours Teen Fandom Event (see chapter 5 for more).

Figure 15. Salt Lake County Library Services ToshoCON (see chapter 5 for more).

Figure 16. Chesterfield County Public Library Comic Con 2015 (see chapter 5 for more).

Figure 17. Homestuck Cosplayers at Chesterfield County Public Library Comic Con 2015 (see chapter 5 for more).

Figure 18. Salt Lake County Library Services Harry Potter Yule Ball (see chapter 5 for more).

Figure 19. DragonCon 2014 Marvel Photo Shoot. *Photo by Wamser Photography*

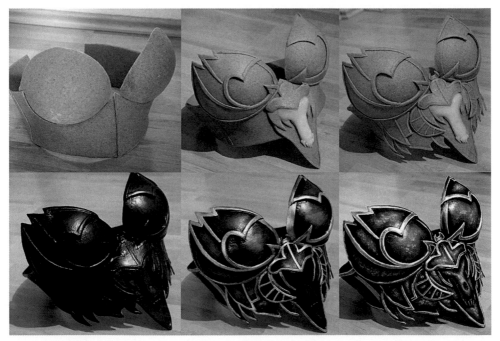

Figure 20. Armor painting, (see chapter 6, project 6 to find out how). *Copyright 2015 by* Kamuicosplay.com

Figure 21. Cosplay cards from Moo.com (see chapter 6, project 10 to find out how). *Gozer photo by Ron Gejon Photography*

Figure 22. Anthony Murray as Steampunk Deadpool and Amy-Lee Cosplay as Ladypool. *Photo by Jeremy Snipe Photography*

Figure 23. Raymundo Grayson as Nightwing. *Photo credit Felix Wong*

Figure 24. Keith Grillman as Wolverine. *Photo by SuperHero Photography by Adam Jay*

Figure 25. Matt Fasanaro as Spider-Man Unlimited and Frankie Koelle as Ben Reilly.

Figure 26. Chris Smith as a member of the Borg Collective (*Star Trek*), CookieCupcakes of *Priority One Podcast* as the TARDIS from *Doctor Who*, Morn from *Star Trek: Deep Space Nine. Photo by Priority One Podcast* http://priorityonepodcast.com

Figure 27. KitKett as anime sailor with Giallo Girl as Jean Grey from the *New X-Men* at Myrtle Beach Comic Con. *Photo by Heroes 4 Hire*

Figure 28. Delta Major as Sailor Moon Neptune from the Sailor Moon series.

Figure 29. Joanna Mari Cosplay as Wonder Woman. *Photo by Howard Levy, HSL Photography*

Figure 30. Kamui Cosplay as a wizard, inspired by the *Diablo* 3 video game. *Copyright 2015 by* Kamuicosplay.com

Figure 31. Frozone from *The Incredibles* by Jibrii Ransom, aka Spectra Marvelous. *Photo credit SF Design*

Figure 32. Giallo Girl as Mercy with Johnny Steele as Cochise from *The Warriors*.

cluded, who are building armor in cramped New York City apartments; so, in other words . . . where there's a will, there's a way! This project is relatively neat until the priming and painting steps. Since it is recommended to use a spray primer as well as spray paints for this project, you will want to make sure that your facilities are well ventilated or else go outside for those steps and spray to your heart's content; just put down some old newspapers or craft paper to avoid a multicolored parking lot.

Ordering Worbla

Worbla can be ordered from many different websites, for example, http://www.cosplaysupplies.com. Depending on your anticipated attendance, it is recommended that you order one to two jumbo sheets of Worbla a few weeks prior to the workshop. Each sheet will measure 39.25" × 59". All other supplies can be found at craft stores such as Michaels or, in the case of the hot air gun, at a home supply store such as Home Depot or Lowe's.

Preparation

You will want to watch a few video tutorials on armor building with Worbla (see chapter 2 for links) in order to familiarize yourself with the process ahead of time. There are also many print tutorials online that you may want to print out as inspiration for the participants. Additionally, it is highly recommended that you have on hand a copy of Kamui Cosplay's *The Book of Cosplay Armor-Making*. This is available in print and also in e-book PDF format for $5 and can be loaded on the instructor's machine for helpful step-by-step illustrations and images. Svetlana Quindt, or Kamui Cosplay, is a recognized expert at armor building with Worbla and other materials and has created some magnificent armor builds. See figures 2 and 30 for photos. The book can be downloaded from her website (http://www.kamuicosplay.com/store).

How to Create Armor Gauntlets

Your workshop can be organized so that participants can choose to make whatever type of armor that they want to create, for example, chestplate, bracers, pauldrons, and so on. However, bear in mind that Worbla is expensive, and you will want to make sure that you have enough for everyone to create something extraordinary in this workshop. So depending on how many attendees you have, you may want to designate a particular armor piece that they can create. I chose gauntlets for this project because not only will they use minimal amounts of Worbla, but, unlike pieces such as a chestplate or pauldrons, they will not need to be fixed to the body via an attachment apparatus. They are also quick to create, so this workshop has the potential to lead participants all the way through to the finishing stage.

Creating the Pattern

Creating a pattern for armor pieces is a process that is a little more art than science. The easiest and most popular way to create personalized armor patterns is to wrap oneself (or at least the part that needs to be patterned) in plastic wrap and then cover the plastic wrap with masking tape. Then use a marker to draw on the masking tape the outline of where the armor will go. Once the pattern has been drawn, the plastic wrap can be cut off of the body and the pattern can be cut out. The pattern is then usually transferred to either craft paper or foam.

To begin, wrap your arm from wrist to elbow in plastic wrap. Cover the entire area with masking tape. Next, decide how far up your arm you want the gauntlet to go. Gauntlets can be short and range from the wrist to halfway to the elbow, or very long and stretch all the way to the elbow. They can be squared off or have a V shape on either or both ends. Think about what you want the shape of your gauntlet to be. When you've decided, take the marker and draw the shape of your gauntlet on the masking tape. Gauntlets do not stretch entirely around the arm; however, they do curve around to the sides of the arm in most cases, so bear this in mind as well. Don't worry about messing up—it's just masking tape and plastic wrap! Additionally, you can always go over your initial pattern with another color if you've made a mistake. When you have your pattern drawn, carefully cut off the plastic wrap on the underside of the arm. Flatten out the wrap and tape to see your pattern, and then carefully cut the pattern out. Transfer your pattern onto a piece of craft foam.[22]

Working with Worbla

Take your pattern piece or your craft foam cutout and place it on the Worbla sheet. Trace the pattern with the marker. With a very sharp pair of scissors, cut out the Worbla piece. Save all of your Worbla scraps; you will need them later. You are now already set to start creating your armor! However, at this point, you'll want to think about whether or not you will want to create two gauntlets. If you do, cut out another piece of craft foam, as you'll be using one for this next step.

Now you will decide whether you want to employ the sandwich method, layering two pattern pieces of Worbla with a layer of craft foam in between for added sturdiness; whether you'll opt for just a single layer of Worbla; or whether you'll go with one piece of Worbla to one piece of craft foam. I have found that the latter—one pattern piece of Worbla to one piece of craft foam—works very well for gauntlets, providing just enough stability while not using too much Worbla, and, additionally, the presence of the craft foam makes it possible to shape the Worbla directly on the arm without burning it. If you'd like to follow this method, start by taking a look at your Worbla pattern piece. One side of the material is rough, while the other is shiny and smooth. The shiny, smooth side is the adhesive side.

Now is the time to put on protective gloves; you will be working with hot Worbla as well as a hot air gun. With the adhesive side facing up, start to heat your pattern piece with the hot air gun. In a minute or two, you will see the material change consistency to look more like putty than hard plastic. Stick the craft foam onto the Worbla. While the Worbla is still hot, pick it up and place it over your forearm and curve it to the shape of your arm like a gauntlet. (**Note:** Even though there is a craft-foam backing, the Worbla will still be hot, so make sure that you are wearing long sleeves!) Keep the Worbla on for a few minutes until it cools. Once cooled, you can pop it off of your arm and you will have a basic gauntlet that will keep its shape indefinitely . . . even in battle!

Creating Details

Round up all of your Worbla scraps that were created when you cut out your pattern pieces. Cut out long stripes, V shapes, and borders to overlay on your gauntlet and create depth and detail. Worbla can be heated up and treated like putty in order to join scraps together and create small details such as leaves and filigree patterns. You can even mold spikes to protrude from your gauntlets.[23] Get creative and mold shapes such as stars, moons, or even hearts on your gauntlets.

Priming and Sanding

Worbla has a very rough surface, and if painted on directly without any priming or sanding, it would look like painted sandpaper. To make it smoother before painting, it is recommended that you cover it using a primer of some sort. One way to go is to apply several (six to ten) coats of Gesso, which is like a thin acrylic paint. However, using Gesso is an extremely time-consuming process as it takes several hours for each coat to dry, and once the final coat is dry it is recommended to wait at least a day before sanding. A faster and more preferable option is to use a spray primer. Spray primers prepare surfaces for painting and take only minutes to dry, so you can apply two to three coats in a very short time frame. Be sure that you are in a well-ventilated space and have covered your area with newspaper or craft paper. Once the primer coats have dried, you will want to sand the surface with sandpaper to make sure that it's smooth.[24] Depending on the length of time you have allotted for your workshop and the pace at which participants have prepared their gauntlets, you may or may not have time to get through sanding; however, you can certainly instruct participants in the process and get them started. They can then take their gauntlets home and continue finishing them, or you can give them the option to return in order to continue to work on them.

Painting

You've primed and sanded your Worbla gauntlets to a smooth surface and you are now ready to paint! The possibilities are endless; however, to begin with, you may want to start off with a base coat of black spray paint followed by a metallic gold or silver over the entire surface of the gauntlet and then use acrylic paints and paintbrushes to fill in the detail work with complementary colors. You may also attempt some weathering and light and shadowing techniques, which can be found in countless YouTube cosplay armor-painting tutorials, as well in Kamui's $5 e-book *The Book of Cosplay Painting* which can be found at http://www.kamuicosplay.com/store.

PROJECT 6: HOW TO HOST AN ARMOR-PAINTING EVENT

Whether you plan to offer the previous workshop on building armor with Worbla or not, a great idea for a follow-up or a stand-alone event is a workshop on how to paint armor. Patrons can bring in projects that they have been working on using Worbla, foam, paper, or any other type of material for this session. This will be an opportunity to teach participants about how to transform their projects through painting and shadowing techniques. See figure 20 for an example.

This step-by-step project was contributed by Svetlana Quindt, aka Kamui Cosplay,[25] a well-known costume and prop designer whose work can be found at http://www.kamuicosplay.com. See figures 2 and 30 to view her remarkable work.

Materials Needed

- Acrylic paint in a variety of colors
- Paint brushes ranging from thin to large
- A well-ventilated space

Building amazing armor requires a bit of artistic skill, a lot of free time, and often a good amount of pocket money. After you've put a lot of blood and sweat into creating a costume—shaping shin guards, helmets, and breastplates—and your creation finally comes together, you realize that only half of the job is done. Since it's very likely that you didn't use real metal to bring a your glorious warrior to life, you will need to give your EVA foam, Worbla, or cardboard a nice paint job to make it look more realistic.

Priming

If you're working with Worbla, don't forget to prime your armor pieces first. Once you've heated up the material, it becomes rough and takes on an almost sand-like texture. Since you mostly want to create a nice, shiny surface, you will have to apply a couple of layers of primer prior to painting. Some layers of Gesso—which is a thick, white acrylic paint—or just simple wood glue is perfect for the job. When using Gesso, make sure to let every layer dry before you apply the next. You can also use a hair dryer to accelerate the process. Keep adding primer layers until you are satisfied with the result. If you are using Gesso, you will also have to sand your layers before you can start painting. Wood glue doesn't require any additional sanding, so it's definitely my preferred method for this step.

Painting

The first thing you should do after priming your material surface is to coat your entire armor piece with a base color. Since this sets the basic color scheme for your entire piece, choose it carefully. There are many different ways to do this step: use an air brush, metallic spray colors, paint by hand, or even get a professional chrome job. The easiest and most straightforward way to work is to use regular acrylic paints that you can find in every well-organized hobby shop. You don't need to be an art student in order to master painting costumes as long as you just follow a few basic principles and are patient with your work. Painting a piece usually takes a little bit longer than building it.

The easiest way to paint with acrylics is from dark to bright. The base color coat should be in the darkest shadow color that you need. Since acrylic colors are very opaque, it's very easy to just add layers of color on top of each other in order to create nice effects. This is the technique we are going to use. Take a color palette and mix different brightnesses of the color you want. I recommend mixing at least three different brightnesses in order to create a nice range of contrast. If you are afraid of making mistakes or are not sure if you like the colors you have, you can always test them on a tiny sample piece first.

Take a big, soft brush and dry it using a towel—we are going to need only a tiny bit of color and very little to no water on the brush. Now take a color that is slightly brighter than your base coat and start dabbing on the surface of your armor piece, beginning in the center. You will notice that the more you dab, the less color will transfer from your brush to the surface. Use this technique in order to create nice gradients from the center to the border of your pieces. This will make them look more three-dimensional and interesting than if you simply applied one brightness of each color. Use this dry-brushing technique in order to create nice shadings very easily without having to be afraid of messing up too much. Now use a slightly brighter variant of your color and repeat the process until you have a nice dark-to-bright gradient of your desired color. I recommend following along the shapes of your built armor piece to find nice shapes that you can fill with color gradients in order to make the paint job fit the overall shape of your piece. This way there will always be shadow near the edges, which will make your piece look very nice.

After you have applied your rough color gradients, switch to a thinner brush and use your darkest shadow color to trace the detail lines of armor pieces again in order to clean up your rough dabbing work a bit. When dabbing with big brushes, there will always be a bit of color that goes where you don't want it, so you will need to clean a bit afterward. When you are done, use a very thin brush with white or another really bright color and add a few very thin highlight lines around your piece. This will make your details pop and help make your piece look even better close up.

Finishing

When you are done with your paint job, you will have to seal it by using either glossy or matte varnish. This will protect your finished work from dust, scratches, and bad weather. Use a brush to apply a thick layer of varnish, or just use spray varnish instead. Once dry, your colors will shine even more vibrantly and will stay like that for a long time.

Kamui's excellent and helpful book *The Book of Cosplay Painting,* as well as others, can be found at http://www.kamuicosplay.com/store.

PROJECT 7: BUDGET COSPLAY EVENT: HOW TO CREATE AN INFINITY GAUNTLET WITH CRAFT FOAM

Hosting a budget cosplay event is a great opportunity for the library not only to offer an affordable program but to teach cosplayers valuable skills that they will be able to use in their future cosplays. Many of the librarians I spoke with in the preparation of this book echoed the same concern, that there were many teens and tweens in their communities who wanted to cosplay but could not afford to do so. They all advised that librarians should have some sort of ancillary activities at cosplay events for those who are just as motivated about the culture but would not financially be able to create a costume.

I have seen many different types of cosplay costumes, some extravagant and some thrown together and still others that were outrageously creative, made from found materials such as pizza boxes and papier-mâché. There are many different options available to cosplayers on a budget. The following three projects (projects 7, 8, and 9) are different cosplay options for building costumes for little or no money.

Creating the Infinity Gauntlet

The Infinity Gauntlet, featured in Marvel Comics, was created by the Titan Thanos by combining six infinity gems on his left gauntlet in order to give him unlimited power over the universe. This gauntlet is instantly recognizable by any comic book fan and can be easily, and cheaply, re-created within a couple of hours. If you're not sure what the Infinity Gauntlet looks like, simply google it and you'll come up with many results, or see figure 4 to see the one that I created.

There are several online tutorials on how to create an Infinity Gauntlet; however, my favorite is the video walkthrough offered by Crabcat Industries—a team of two women, Jessica Merizan and Holly Conrad, who design and build props and costumes. They have been featured on *Heroes of Cosplay* and host a web series called *Try This at Home!* on their website, http://crabcatindustries.com/, which features tutorial episodes for everything from how to build puppets to how to build a DeLorean Time Machine. It is their video tutorial that this project will be based on; however, it will be modified slightly. Please see the video here https://www.youtube.com/watch?v=8z4Lc98gadE or here http://tinyurl.com/m3rkw42.

Materials Needed

- Scissors
- Latex dishwashing gloves—$2
- One to two sheets of craft foam—$2
- Superglue—$4
- Glass gems in multiple colors (found in the floral department of Michaels)—$3
- Gold metallic spray paint—$5
- Plasti Dip black rubber coating spray—$6
- Total cost: $22 (however, you can likely make two gloves with just these supplies!)

Assembling the Gauntlet

The gauntlet is going to be the part that goes on your arm, from wrist to elbow. To start off, simply wrap a piece of craft foam around your arm to see how much you will need for a gauntlet. You will want to try and make the wrist end smaller and narrower than the elbow end, which you'll want to flare out a bit. Bear in mind, however, that you'll be wanting to attach another piece to the wrist as well as fit your glove through it later, so don't make it too tight. When you've got the shape, cut off the excess and superglue it together. The Crabcat team suggests using Barge contact cement, which can be quite toxic as well as very pricey; however, the same results can be achieved by using superglue or hot glue, whichever you prefer. At the elbow end of the gauntlet, glue several square pieces of foam as well as a narrow strip to form a border along the edge in order to give the gauntlet more depth.

Next you'll want to create the hand piece of the gauntlet. For this, cut a rectangular piece of foam that fits around your hand and from your wrist to your knuckles and glue the ends together. You can then cut a circular hole in this piece for your gloved thumb to go through. This will be how the gauntlet stays on your hand. Glue this piece just inside of the wrist section of the larger gauntlet. Now you've got a gauntlet assembled. For an added detail, cut a strip of foam for a border between the two sections of the gauntlet.

Finally, you'll want to create places on your gauntlet for your Infinity Gems to rest. For that, you can cut out a curved foam piece that can be glued over the knuckle portion of the gauntlet. This piece can be topped with four foam circles—one for each knuckle—on which you will later rest the stones. You'll also want to cut out one extra circle, which will be glued to your gloved thumb knuckle. And last, cut out a large foam circle for the one slightly larger gem that will be placed in the center of the hand portion of the gauntlet. Glue all of these foam pieces onto the gauntlet. If the placement isn't clear, take a look at figure 4 and/or the video. Don't place any of the stones on the gauntlet at this point.

Creating the Glove

The next part of the project involves creating a glove to fit inside of the gauntlet. Take one of the latex dishwashing gloves and put it on. For the glove, you'll want to build up the knuckles and the fingertips to make it look more like it is being worn by a Titan. To do this, simply cut some narrow strips of foam to cover your finger knuckles and fingertips. The foam doesn't need to go all the way around the knuckles, but you'll definitely want it to fold it over each knuckle and you can trim off the excess. To glue these pieces on, I would highly recommend using superglue as I've found that very few glues actually stay stuck onto latex. Hot glue simply hardened and then popped off for me, and white glue was a disaster. Once you're finished bulking up the knuckles, you can move on to covering the fingertips, which involves a bit of finessing. You'll want to cut out strips that have a middle part to fold over the fingertip; in order to achieve this, cut the foam pieces in a kind of a T shape. Crabcat Industries has a great image of what they call "finger cups" on their website: http://crabcatindustries.com/2012/10/visual-aids-the-infinity-gauntlet. At this point, the glove is nearly ready; simply glue that final foam circle onto the thumb knuckle area where you will attach a gem after painting.

Painting

You are now ready to paint both the glove and gauntlet. Be sure to put down newspapers or craft paper and make sure that you are in a well-ventilated space. To start out, the tutorial video recommends using a coat of 3M Hi-Strength 90 Spray Adhesive at $14 a can. I skipped this step as I didn't want to make that investment and found it unnecessary. I went right to the coat of Plasti Dip, which coats the foam and latex glove in a thin layer of black rubber, thus sealing it. You can apply as many coats of Plasti Dip as you'd like; I used only one. After it's dry (I only gave my project about a half an hour to dry, but it will depend on the temperature and how thick the coat is, among other variables), you can spray on the gold spray paint and it instantly looks like an Infinity Gauntlet! All that's left is to wait for the paint to dry (most spray paint dries in a matter of minutes) and glue on the glass gems with a little bit of superglue.

Once everything is dry, carefully slip the glove inside of the gauntlet; this is probably easiest to do without the glove on. Then you will put on the gauntlet and take it off, keeping the glove inside of the gauntlet. **Warning:** This is a replica of the Infinity Gauntlet and promises no omnipotent powers over the universe!

PROJECT 8: BUDGET COSPLAY EVENT: HOW TO CREATE CARDBOARD SUPERHERO HELMETS

There are countless online tutorials for how to create superhero and other helmets from simple cardboard. See figure 3 for an excellent example of a Judge Dredd helmet created with cardboard. Additionally, there are many Pepakura patterns not only for Iron Man's helmet but for his entire suit for anyone who wants to start out with a pattern to use on card stock or even to use with the cardboard. This is a great opportunity for the library to introduce Pepakura, the practice of folding card stock or paper to create cosplay costumes and props (see chapter 2 for more details and figures 5 and 6 for examples). You can show participants the Pepakura gallery (http://www.tamasoft.co.jp/pepakura-en) and explain how, with simple card stock or cardboard and a little (okay, a lot!) of patience, they can build incredible costumes.

How to Build an Iron Man Helmet from Five Pieces of Cardboard

Cardboard Iron Man helmets are fairly popular undertakings, so you'll find many tutorials available online; however, the best and easiest one that I've found is Dustin McLean's do-it-yourself (DIY) cardboard Iron Man helmet video in which he walks the viewer through exactly how to create his or her own helmet with just five pieces of cardboard. His excellent video can be found at https://www.youtube.com/watch?v=Cf-Q12XaTVM.

McLean not only provides exact measurements and instructions but also the reference/pattern images, which you can download here:

- Faceplate: http://imgur.com/RBO4Kkz
- Jaw: http://imgur.com/FTZDZgc
- Sides: http://imgur.com/fpf7SZM
- Top: http://imgur.com/K2B0gwC

Materials Needed

- Ruler
- Permanent marker
- Scissors
- Hot glue gun
- Cardboard
- Glue sticks—$4
- Red spray paint—$5
- Gold spray paint—$5
- Total cost (if tools are already owned): $14

Preparing for the Workshop

In order to prepare for this event, you will want to print out the pattern pieces, trace them onto cardboard, and cut out an example set of pieces for participants to trace and use while designing their own helmets. Watch the video to see how the pieces are glued together or even show it during the workshop. Help attendees get their pieces glued; then they will be ready to paint. Since most spray paint dries in no time—or in a matter of about ten minutes—participants can easily complete this project within the time frame of a library workshop.

Alternative Helmets

You may want to offer participants the opportunity to create cardboard helmets other than Iron Man if they have another favorite that they'd rather build for a cosplay. You can find numerous other tutorials online and some even have alternative patterns at the ready, such as:

- How to make a cardboard Boba Fett helmet (includes templates): http://www.instructables.com/id/How-to-make-a-cardboard-costume-helmet/?ALLSTEPS
- How to make a cardboard *Halo 4* Master Chief helmet by TheMachinga: https://www.youtube.com/watch?v=rNvvJBg1F7c

Dali DIY's channel on YouTube (https://www.youtube.com/user/dali1lomo) offers more than ninety tutorial videos. All of the video projects come complete with free template/pattern files for creating many pop culture and superhero helmets from cardboard and papier-mâché coating to make them sturdier. This makes it easy for you to choose a couple of alternative helmets for participants to create and print out their pattern files ahead of time.

The Dali DIY channel is very popular, with over five million views and forty thousand subscribers. Many of these projects can get quite involved, however, so you'll want to be sure to watch the videos beforehand to decide if you'd like to offer an abbreviated version of the project. But they are sure to be crowd-pleasers.

- Storm Troopers
- Magneto (*X-Men*)
- Power Rangers
- Star Lord (*Guardians of the Galaxy*)
- Batman
- Spiderman
- Wolverine (*X-Men*)

Finishing Basics

Cardboard helmets can be finished by directly spray painting them; however, I would like to point out that there are other methods that cosplayers use to finish their cardboard and Pepakura (paper) cosplays, and helmets in particular. Some will use papier-mâché in order to offer an added layer of durability. If the helmet or prop was created using paper, cosplayers will often cure it afterward with Modgepodge, white glue, or else some type of resin in order to stiffen and seal the paper. Fiberglass resin is most often used, but it is quite toxic and necessitates that a respirator, protective eye gear, and gloves be worn. Additionally, it should really be used outside due to the lingering fumes. Epoxy resin is a less toxic alternative to fiberglass resin, although once again, Modgepodge can be used. (For a more thorough explanation on resin types and Pepakura, this is a very informative video: https://www.youtube.com/watch?v=eJmB0yw3sOY.) Following this curing stage, many cosplayers will apply Bondo automotive body filler to their creations. This hardens the entire helmet or prop piece and smooths it. The Bondo layer is then usually sanded down before painting. Some cosplayers will also use automotive paints to finish their helmets due to their high-gloss sheen.

PROJECT 9: BUDGET COSPLAY EVENT: HOW TO CREATE PAPIER-MÂCHÉ MINIONS

The last form of budget cosplay that I would like to suggest for an event or workshop is the art of papier-mâché. Many cosplayers use this craft form in order to create face masks and props, add a sturdy layer to Pepakura projects, or even create monsters and minions to accompany their cosplays. As I mentioned in chapter 2, I was very successful with this craft form when I needed to figure out a way to have a very large Terror Dog monster to accompany my Gozer *Ghostbusters* cosplay. (See figure 7 for a photo.) This is an incredibly easy craft form to learn and can be used in any number of ways. Best of all, it is essentially a free way to create something from just about nothing, as most people have old newspapers, flour, and water on hand.

Materials Needed

- A stack of newspapers
- Flour
- Water
- Paintbrushes
- Scissors
- Hot glue gun
- Glue sticks—$4
- Optional: an old sheet and white glue
- Premo! Sculpey polymer clay—$3
- Masking tape—$1
- Latex or acrylic paints in various colors—$5–$15
- Total cost: $13–$23

Creating Your Minions

There are many guides on how to create papier-mâché props and even monsters; however, the one that I found the most helpful when creating my Terror Dog was Dan Reeder's *Papier-Mâché Monsters: Turn Trinkets and Trash into Magnificent Monstrosities.*[26] This is a step-by-step instructional guidebook with many illustrative images to walk you through each step in the process. The Kindle edition can be purchased for just $7.50, and I highly recommend it for libraries that are interested in teaching papier-mâché workshops. What I would suggest for a first workshop is a simplified version of Reeder's "monster" consisting of a head, ears, body, and tail. The disadvantage to papier-mâché projects is the time you must wait for the craft to dry, so you want to be sure that the first project that participants undertake isn't too technically difficult so that they feel that the project was a success.

To start off, what you will want to do is crumple up newspapers and form them into a head-shaped ball about the size of a grapefruit. Place some masking tape around the ball in order to keep its shape and set it aside. Create another, much larger ball to be used as a body. It is okay if they are disproportionate; these are supposed to be monsters. Next create two small balls that will be cut in half later on in order to create ears. And finally, create a tail-shaped form from crumpled newspapers and masking tape.

Papier-Mâché

For this next stage, take a bunch of newspapers and tear them into long, narrow strips, which will be used to wrap your minion. You're now ready to start preparing your papier-mâché mixture. Simply take flour and water and mix them in a large bowl until the consistency becomes that of paste, or as Dan refers to it, that of "thick soup." Wet your hands with the paste mixture and then take a strip of newspaper, wet it with your hands, and place it on the first ball, making sure that it is soaked through as you wrap it around. Add the next newspaper strip and repeat the process until the ball is covered and soaked with newspaper strips and paste. Continue the same procedure with all of your shapes. At this point, you will need to let your papier-mâché pieces dry before assembly and painting. This will most likely take at least twenty-four hours.

Making Monster Teeth

Perhaps as part 2 of a workshop series, you could invite participants back to work on their minions. A technique that I really liked from Dan's book, and one that I used when creating my own minion, was cutting the head ball shape in half in order to create two parts of a jaw. If you cut the head ball in half and remove the extra crumpled newspapers that are inside of it, you will have two halves of a jaw. You can then take the Sculpey clay and create small, pointy teeth. Sculpt a bunch of these teeth and put them in an oven, following the package instructions. At this point, you might also sculpt two large balls to use for eyes. You can then hot glue the eyes to your minion's head/jaw. You are now ready to assemble the jaw onto your minion's body, but you may consider prepainting the inside of the mouth first, since it will be hard to reach once it's all glued together.

Assembling the Monster

First take the body-shaped ball and cut a head-sized hole in it. Don't worry about messing up; you can always add more masking tape or papier-mâché later. Use the masking tape to fix your head/jaws to the body. Now find the ear-shaped balls and cut them in half and in half again in order to shape them into monster ears. Masking tape the ears onto the head. Ambitious participants can use the scraps from the ear balls to make a nose. Hot glue or tape the eyes into place on the head. Last, attach the tail to the body by poking a small hole in the back of the body, pushing the tailpiece in, and taping it into place.

Cloth Mâché

At this stage you have the choice if you want to add another layer of mâché to the monster to add durability. This can be done by using a similar technique called cloth mâché. With this craft form, you tear an old sheet into strips and dip them directly into a bowl of white glue and then wrap your monster in them. This will then need to dry overnight as well. You could also use a technique discussed in the previous project and brush the entire monster with Modgepodge to coat it.

Painting

Latex paint is recommended for this project in the book; however, I used acrylics, since that's what I had on hand. I found that this worked fairly well, although I had to thin the paint down a bit with water. This is the most fun portion of the project as far as I'm concerned, because it's when you get to see your papier-mâché minion really come to life. Be creative with your color choices as these are not supposed to come from nature!

This is a very abbreviated take on how to create a papier-mâché minion; for the full version, as well as inspiration for creating dragons, bats, and Halloween monsters, be sure to check out Dan Reeder's book![27]

PROJECT 10: HOW TO HOST A COSPLAY CARDS WORKSHOP

Meishi koukan, or the exchange of business cards, is very important among Japanese, as well as American, cosplayers. It is a way of introducing oneself at cons and cosplay events and is a vital form of promotion and networking in the cosplay community.[28] In Japan, there are specialized cosplay business card printers, such as Proof (https://proof.jigmy.com), that will print out calling cards with a cosplayer's contact information, cosplay name, and social networking sites—most often including their address on Cure, the most popular Japanese online cosplay community (http://en.curecos.com).[29] Proof also allows cosplayers to print out multiple photos featuring different costumes in one business card pack for affordable prices.[30] Luckily, there is a similar service available to cosplayers in the United States and Europe, which actually delivers worldwide—a British-born company called Moo.com. I've been ordering from them since their start-up days in 2006, so I can recommend them highly. See figure 21 for a photo.

Many cosplayers are still in their teens and tweens and haven't yet had a professional job that necessitates having business cards and, therefore, have little idea where to begin with creating, designing, and ordering their own. This is where the library can really step in and help out by hosting a workshop that will lead cosplayers through the process of designing their own cosplay calling cards.

Preparing for the Workshop

You will want to reserve the computer lab for a forty-five-minute workshop and suggest that cosplayers come prepared with high-resolution images on flash drives if possible, although this is not absolutely necessary.

Creating Cosplay Cards

I would suggest using Moo.com's Original MiniCards for this project, which are located at http://us.moo.com/products/minicards.html. MiniCards are half the size (lengthwise) of regular business cards, so they really catch the eye and are surprisingly still quite different than the usual size, even after all this time that the product has been available. My MiniCards are always greeted with admiration for their uniqueness and also for the high quality of the card stock used in their production. And they are also quite affordable for cosplayers. A pack of one hundred double-sided MiniCards costs only $19.99, and you are able to use as many images as you'd like in your order. If you wish, you could create an order of cards with one hundred different photos on them, making each business card unique.

To get started, each workshop participant will want to create an account on Moo.com. Once the participant is signed in, he or she will navigate to Products → MiniCards → Original MiniCards. From here, you will have two choices.

Design Your Own

This easy option will lead you through a wizard that will allow you to effortlessly design your pack of one hundred double-sided MiniCards. You begin by clicking on the front side of the card. This is where you add your contact information and any text that you want. **Note:** The interface suggests many different lines to fill out with information, but these are only suggestions and guidelines. On my own cards, I only have two lines of text, which I center on the card by typing on the third and fourth lines, where it is suggested to enter your mailing address and e-mail address. Instead of these addresses, I type my cosplay name—Giallo Girl—on the third line, center the text, and make the font larger (10.5 pt), bold, and hot pink. On the fourth line, I enter my cosplay Facebook page—http://www.facebook.com/giallogirl—and I center the text, bold it, and make the font larger (9.5 pt). Then I'm finished. At this stage in the workshop, you might discuss what types of information are appropriate to list on business cards and what information cosplayers may not want to give out, such as their phone number, and so on.

Next is the fun part. Choosing your photos. Clicking on the back side of the card will bring up a dialog box that will let you access the photos on your local computer via the Upload Images option. You will also be able to upload any photos that you have in galleries on many different social networking websites, including Instagram, Facebook, Flickr, SmugMug, and Etsy. Clicking on any one of these choices will walk you through logging into the application and then allow you to choose which images to use on your Moo.com MiniCards. Simply drag the images that you want to use into the Moo interface and choose "Add to Image Slot" in order to add them to your card pack. You can then use Moo's tools to adjust the images to fit your cards. To continue to add additional images, simply click on the plus (+) sign on the top right. Moo will keep count of how many of each photo you will get in your pack as you go. If you decide you don't like an image that you've added to your card pack, just click on the trash can icon on the top right to "remove side." On the top right menu, you always have the options to save your project or start again.

Upload a Complete Design

Moo.com also allows you to create custom graphics for your MiniCards and then upload those designs directly for use on the cards. If you chose this option, you will be led to a page with custom templates providing artwork guidelines for designing your cards. These files are available in Photoshop, Illustrator, and InDesign file types, as well as in .jpg format. If you choose to allow your workshop participants to use this option, you will want to explain to them the concept of a bleed area in designing artwork—the background area that you want to extend further than your actual desired image in order to keep your cards from having unsightly white edges when they are trimmed. You will also want to underscore the importance of keeping all of the vital areas of the images within the "safe area" in order to keep them from being cut off with the trim. Once the templates are opened in an image-editing application such as Photoshop, it is quite easy to paste your images directly over the template in separate layers to ensure they stay within the safe area of the card. Some background or instruction in using an image-editing program is necessary, however, so you'll need to decide whether or not to include this option in your workshop.

Why might you want to do this? For me, personally, I use this option because I want to have cards with each one showing multiple photos of my cosplays. I create an image that has five different cosplay photos on it, divided by black borders (see figure 21). I use the provided template to make sure that my custom design is within the image guidelines and won't be trimmed too much. I then use my design as a template and update it each year with new cosplay photos. I often upload two or three of these designs to include in my pack, which allows me to have ten to fifteen different cosplay photos printed on those two to three designs. If you choose this option, and if you are comfortable with the artwork guidelines, click on "I'm Ready" on the bottom-right side of the page to get started. You will then be able to upload your file. Unfortunately, Moo.com requires that you upload complete design files for both the front and back of the card. You can also just use this interface to see how your custom design came out and how it will look when trimmed. I prefer to use the Moo.com wizard interface for the details or front side of my card, so I use their custom templates to design my artwork for the back sides of my Moo MiniCards and then I upload them using the first option—"Design Your Own."

Whichever option you chose, you should now have designed your own pack of Moo Mini-Cards. At this point, it is a good idea to download or e-mail yourself a PDF proofsheet so that you know exactly what you're getting before you place your order. You should take a good look to see if any editing needs to be done before moving on. You then have the choice to either save this as a project for later or add the cards to your cart and order them.

PROJECT 11: HOST A COSPLAY WEB PRESENCE WORKSHOP

The most common way that cosplayers build up their reputations in the community is by setting up a Facebook page for their cosplay photos and activities. But what should cosplayers include on such a page? What about privacy? And what other social media do cosplayers employ in order to get "likes" and exposure? Libraries can help with these questions and more by offering helpful workshops on how to create a cosplay web presence. Here are the details that you will want to be sure to cover in your session.

What Are the Benefits of Having a Cosplay Facebook Page?

A Facebook page is a place where you can post about what you're working on, interact with fans, view metrics and statistics, advertise and promote your page and your posts, and create a community.

- Facebook pages have analytics that give metrics about who is using and interacting with your page, including: total page likes (or a number of fans), daily active users, new likes, like sources, demographics, page views, individual tab views, external referrers, post reach and engagement, including likes, comments, shares, and clicks.
- Facebook pages have advertising and post promotion options.
- Facebook pages allow you to add social plugins and "like" buttons to other websites in order to draw traffic.
- Facebook pages are public and fully indexed by search engines.
- There are no friend limits on Facebook pages. (There's a five-thousand-friend limit on profiles.)
- Facebook pages have community building tools such as the "invite friends" feature.

How to Set Up a Cosplay Facebook Page

Creating a business page on Facebook is quite easy, simply click the "Create Page" option from the main menu and choose "Artist, Band or Public Figure" from the choices provided. (**Note:** Facebook constantly makes changes to their interface, so the exact placement of the option may change, but it will always be available.) You will then need to choose a category. The most popular categories used by cosplayers for their pages are "artist" or "public figure." However, some do opt for "entertainer" or "actor," depending on their career aspirations. Once you've decided on a category, choose a name for your page, and you're off! It's helpful to note that most cosplayers do not use their real names for their pages or for their cosplay activity but instead operate under a pseudonym or professional name. This helps protect their privacy and also adds a bit of fun to their personas.

Now that you've created your cosplay page, what should you do next? Well, you should definitely start posting some relevant status updates and uploading photos to albums. But first, let's talk about privacy and making sure that you maintain control of your message.

Settings and Privacy

A link to your settings page will appear in the upper-right-hand corner of your page. Click on it and look at all of the different privacy settings that Facebook allows you to control in the left navigation menu. Some key areas to be sure to be aware of and in some cases adjust are discussed below.

General

There are quite a few general settings that you can adjust on your page. Two of these areas, posting ability and tagging ability, affect your page in major ways.

- *Posting Ability.* Here is where you will set how and what people can post on your page. It is highly recommended that you moderate all of the posts made on your page timeline before they are made public in order to avoid spam and inappropriate posts. Look at the current settings. The first two should be left as they appear in the default setting: "Anyone can post to my page timeline" and "Anyone can add photos and videos to my page timeline." However, you will want to make sure that there is a third setting in this area that reads "Posts by other users will be moderated." If that does not appear, click the "Edit" option and check "Review posts by other people before they are shown on my page." This will keep control of what goes on your wall firmly in your hands.
- *Tagging Ability.* By default, only the page administrators have permission to tag people in photos that you post. However, you will want people to be able to tag themselves and their friends when they appear in your photos to increase the exposure of and engagement with your page. To change this setting, click the "Edit" option and choose "Allow others to tag photos and videos posted by [*yourpagename*]."

Notifications

Here is where you can choose how you would like to be notified about comments, page mentions, page likes, and so on. You may want to receive a notification for each of these events as they occur or receive notification of activity in digest form every twelve to twenty-four hours. Facebook gives you the ability to get very granular about these settings.

Activity Log

The last area of note in the settings section is quite important. It is your activity log, which not only gives you a list of what everyone else did on your page but also lists actions that you yourself took. This is where you can easily adjust privacy settings on individual posts, photos, notes, and other items. You can set the privacy to be public (the default for pages) or restrict it to a subset of people or just yourself. You can also easily delete posts and activity here to keep them from appearing on your timeline. To make things easier, you can separate and view different kinds of activities with the left-hand filters. There is also a search box available.

Insights

The next major section of your page is the insights area with all of your statistics about traffic and site usage. Click on the Insights menu item on the top of your page.

The **overview** area will give you a snapshot of how many page likes you have received as well as what type of reach and engagement people have had with your posts during the last week. Scrolling down, you will have a list of your most recent posts, as well as the details about their individual reach, engagement, likes, comments, and shares. At this point, a couple of definitions are necessary:

- **Post reach:** the number of people your post was served to.
- **Post engagement:** the number of actions such as likes, comments, clicks, and shares that occurred on your posts.

Clicking across the top menu options in the insights area will allow you to see more details about likes, reach, visits, posts, and people. These statistics pages will enable you to designate date ranges to track page activity. These areas have crucial information that can help inform you about when you should publish your posts, what types of posts and photos perform best, as well as where your traffic is coming from. Here are some particular areas of note:

- The **visits** tab will provide you with information about external referrers to your page, or what websites led people to your Facebook page the most.
- The **posts** tab will provide you with the most popular times of day that fans of your page are online. This will help inform the best, most optimal time for your posts to deploy on a regular basis in order to reach the most users.
- The **post types** tab within the **posts** area will let you know what types of posts are the most popular with your fans—photos, links, or status updates—and will provide you with a list of your best, most popular posts.

About

This is the area where you can provide people with a brief description of who you are as a cosplayer, as well as a link to your cosplay website or portfolio page, if you have one. This area allows you to provide many different types of information about yourself, which is both a benefit and a drawback. You want to be cautious about how much personal information you provide in this area because all of it will be publicly available. Therefore, you probably will not want to give out your real name here, and you definitely do not want to list your address or your phone number or even an e-mail address—instead, people can contact you through your Facebook inbox. Use this area to link to your cosplay website, your Twitter account, and other social media profiles that you have set up.

Photos

Now comes the fun part! Photos are a very important element of a cosplayer's web presence. Upload photos into albums themed by cosplay character or by event. Choose the best of your photos for your page. You don't have to upload all of them, perhaps just the best five or seven of each costume in an album; if you are spotted at an event and photographed, you can tag yourself in those as well. Post progress photos on your timeline of future cosplays that you're working on as well in order to keep your fans updated. Don't forget that these photos will be public, and always bear that in mind when choosing content.

Posts

What types of things should you post about on your page? The best way to decide is to think about your page as an extension of your brand image that you want to convey. What type of impression do you want to give your fans? Here are some suggestions:

- Post about your cosplay activities—conventions you'll be attending, local events you'll be making appearances at, publications your photos have appeared in, and so on.
- Support other cosplayers in the community by linking to their pages.
- Post photos of conventions that you have attended.
- Show a little personality! How about video games you're playing, movies you've seen or are looking forward to, and so on.
- Ask questions and advice of your community—after all, they're your audience!

Facebook pages have a unique feature that enables you to save drafts of your updates to post at a future time. By selecting the arrow beside the "Post" button, you can choose to save a draft, schedule your post to deploy at a time and date that you set, or even backdate an update.

How to Create and Publish Notes

Creating notes documents on Facebook pages is not very intuitive. You can access notes from the "More" drop-down menu directly underneath your page's cover photo. From there, you can select "Notes" and you will be brought to the notes page where you can click "+Write Note" in order to create a new note. However, the first time you attempt to access notes, this option may not be there. If there is no direct link to notes, you can click "Manage Tabs" and add the Notes app. After adding the app, it will always appear on the "More" menu.

How to Add Events

You can use the exact same method to access and add the Events app to your page. Once Events has been added, you can set up formal events that your fans can share with their friends, RSVP to attend, and post photos, updates, and conversations. This is a great way to keep fans informed about upcoming events and cons that you'll be attending and to get them to come along with you.

Adding, Editing, and Removing Tabs

While in this same area, you can click again on "Manage Tabs" directly underneath your cover photo. Click on "More" → "Manage Tabs" in order to add, remove, or reorder the position of the tabs on your page.

Vanity URLs

Once your page has reached the twenty-five "likes" milestone, you have the option of choosing a custom URL. This is great for your brand and also gives you a very short, easily memorized URL that you can tell people to visit, rather than a string of numbers after "facebook.com." The URL can only be changed once, so think carefully about what you want it to be. You can claim your personalized Facebook URL here: http://www.facebook.com/username.

Page and Link Promotion

Facebook offers many ways to promote and market Facebook pages, as well as your cosplay website if you listed one in the "About" section. From the timeline view of your page, there is a "Promote Your Page" link on the left-hand side, as well as a "Promote" menu on the right, which will enable you to promote your page or your website or access the Ads Manager dashboard to view all of your campaigns. You can easily create an ad for your page just by clicking the "Promote Page" link. This brings up the "Create Ad" dialog box, which is loaded with a suggested ad preview. You also have the option to upload your own artwork as an alternative. Here you can choose which countries will receive the ad, as well as four to ten interest areas that will be targeted. You can even specify whether you want your ad to be served to men or women. Choose a daily budget for your ad and an end date and you're all set. Facebook will provide you with an estimate of how many likes you will probably receive per day as a result of placing the ad.

You can also promote individual posts that you make on your page by clicking the "Boost Post" option below the post. With individual posts, you can choose to serve the ad to only your fans who like your page, to your fans plus their friends, or to a specified audience based on gender, age, location, or areas of interest.

Submitting Your Page to Cosplay Publications

A great (and free!) way to promote your cosplay page is to submit it to some of the many cosplay publications and Facebook pages. There are quite a few online magazines and Facebook pages that accept submissions for their cosplay spotlight or to post on their timelines. I have included a lengthy list of these resources in appendix E, "Cosplay Websites and Blogs Directory." Be sure to read the submission instructions for each as they may vary.

Cross-Channel Promotion

Another very effective way to advertise your Facebook page is to promote it on all of the other social media profiles that you use for your cosplay, such as Twitter, Instagram, DeviantArt, Model Mayhem, your website portfolio, and so on. You may consider any of these social networks as additional places to post your photos, status updates, convention dates, and other items. By having these additional profiles (as long as they're kept up to date!), you can spread the word about your Facebook page to an even wider audience without the fees involved with Facebook ads.

Some Final Facebook Tips

- Use the same profile image in order to maintain consistency across social networks.
- Have your profile reflect your personality, but remember that we don't need to know everything!
- Claim your vanity URL.
- Post your Facebook page URL everywhere—your website, Twitter, and so on.
- Don't ever list your phone number, address, date of birth, or other information that could be used to steal your identity.

- Create events to publicize your cosplay activities.
- Like other people's pages.
- Make comments on other people's status updates.
- Reply to fan comments.
- The bottom line is—be involved!

PROJECT 12: PLAN A THEMED COSPLAY LOCK-IN

After-hours library lock-in events are a big draw for teens, who relish the idea of having free rein to socialize and act silly with their friends in the library. Why not plan a themed cosplay lock-in event similar to those held at the ELANCO and Burlington County Libraries? (See figures 12–14 for photos.) These are low-cost, low-maintenance events that are sure to draw teens from your library's community and beyond. They are a great way to introduce new teens to your library and get your existing teen patrons even more engaged with the organization.

Permission Slips

First off, you will want to make sure that you have parental permission for each teen who wants to take part in the library's lock-in event. It is also a good idea to print up the permission slip with the top portion explaining the program of events, listing any films or anime shorts that may be shown during the event so that any objections can be dealt with beforehand rather than after the fact. These events are always less stressful if all of your bases are covered.[31]

Theme Ideas

These events can be planned around a specific theme in order to give cosplayers some direction as to what types of costumes to create and wear to the event. Below are some themes to consider.

- Literary characters
- Comics
- Anime
- Zombies
- Video games

   Specific fandoms:

- *Doctor Who*
- *Firefly*
- *Star Trek*
- *Star Wars*

Alternatively, the lock-in could be timed to coincide with or precede a particular event that will be popular with cosplayers. Costumes could then be specifically focused in order to be relevant to those events. Some examples might be Free Comic Book Day (the first Saturday in May each year), International Cosplay Day (the last Saturday in August each year), or the releases of these upcoming popular films:

1. Marvel
   - *Captain America: Civil War*—May 6, 2016
   - *Doctor Strange*—November 4, 2016
   - *Guardians of the Galaxy 2*—May 5, 2017
   - *Thor: Ragnarok*—November 3, 2017
   - *Avengers: Infinity War, Part 1*—May 4, 2018
   - *Black Panther*—July 6, 2018
   - *Captain Marvel*—November 2, 2018
   - *Avengers: Infinity War, Part 2*—May 3, 2019[32]
   - *Inhumans*—July 12, 2019[33]
2. DC
   - *Batman v Superman: Dawn of Justice*—March 25, 2016
   - *Suicide Squad*—August 5, 2016
   - *Wonder Woman*—June 23, 2017
   - *Justice League*—November 17, 2017
   - *The Flash*—March 23, 2018
   - *Aquaman*—July 27, 2018
   - *Shazam*—April 5, 2019
   - *Justice League 2*—June 14, 2019
   - *Cyborg*—April 3, 2020
   - *Green Lantern*—June 19, 2020[34]
3. Disney
   - *Star Wars: Episode VII*—December 18, 2015
   - *Star Wars: Episode VIII*—May 26, 2017
   - *Star Wars: Episode IX*—2019[35]

Snacks

The possibilities here are endless, and this leaves a lot of room to get creative. Why not try to make your snacks match your theme? If you will be having an anime-themed lock-in, go to an Asian supermarket and check out all of the wonderful snacks that they have available, including Pocky, Hello Panda cookies, jelly candies, and more. This might be a chance for teens to try some foods that they've never had before. When in doubt, potato chips and pizza are always crowd-pleasers. You might also pick up a healthy option, such as a fruit plate.

Activities

This is an opportunity to combine many different elements from the previous projects and case studies into one event. Take a look through this chapter and select your favorite project elements or the activities that you think will be the most popular among your cosplaying teens and combine them for a stellar lock-in event! Here are some examples:

Project 1: Host a Comic or Anime Con in Your Library!

There are currently over three hundred cosplay photo studios in Japan today,[36] such as Booty (http://bootyjapan.jp/honkan), which features unique sets designed specifically for cosplayers to shoot photos in. Check out the sections in project 1 on "Cosplay Photo Shoots" and "Photo Booths and Backdrops." A cosplay lock-in would be a great time for teens to get creative and create their own sets.

Additionally, you may want to have a theme-appropriate movie playing in the background of your event or an anime episode or two streaming from Crunchyroll or a similar website. Be sure to check out this project's discussion of movie screenings and licensing.

Project 2: Host a Cosplay Contest

Many cosplayers enjoy the opportunity to show off their hard work on their costumes, and a costume contest is just such a showcase. Prizes are optional and don't have to be expensive to represent appreciation. You could easily integrate this type of event into a library lock-in.

Project 3: Form a Cosplay Club

Cosplay clubs, similar to any other teen clubs such as anime, book, or video game clubs, have a wide range of activities at their meetings. Take another look at this project to get ideas and inspiration for icebreakers, games, and activities to host at your gathering.

Projects 4–11: Hands-On Workshop Events

Hands-on workshop events are always popular with teens, who enjoy being taught how to create new things, learn new skills, and take home their creations afterward. Why not combine one of these interactive instructional workshops into your library's lock-in? Projects to consider include:

- Project 4: A Cosplay Props 3-D Printing Event
- Project 5: A Create-Your-Own Armor with Worbla Event
- Project 6: Cosplay Armor Painting
- Project 7: How to Create an Infinity Gauntlet with Craft Foam
- Project 8: How to Create Cardboard Superhero Helmets
- Project 9: How to Create Papier-Mâché Minions
- Project 10: A Cosplay Business Cards Workshop
- Project 11: A Cosplay Web Presence Workshop

Sample Schedules of Events

You have many options at your disposal for organizing these events. Here are just some ideas of what your program might look like.

A Cosplay Library Lock-In
- 6:30 p.m.–7:00 p.m. Teens arrive in costume
- 7:00 p.m.–7:30 p.m. Icebreaker activities and snacks
- 7:30 p.m.–8:30 p.m. Cosplay contest
- 8:30 p.m.–9:00 p.m. Cosplay photo shoots

A Library Zombie Prom Lock-In
- 6:30 p.m.–7:00 p.m. Teens arrive in Zombie costumes
- 7:00 p.m.–8:00 p.m. Cosplay crafting and snacks

- 8:00 p.m.–8:45 p.m. "Thriller" dance-off
- 8:45 p.m.–9:00 p.m. Group photo shoot

Avengers Assemble! A Marvel Comics Library Lock-In
- 6:30 p.m.–7:00 p.m. Teens arrive in Marvel Comics costumes
- 7:00 p.m.–7:30 p.m. Icebreaker Name That Superhero trivia game and snacks
- 7:30 p.m.–8:30 p.m. Teens build Infinity Gauntlets with craft foam
- 8:30 p.m.–9:00 p.m. Cosplay parade

An Animazing Library Lock-In
- 6:30 p.m.–7:00 p.m. Teens arrive in anime costumes
- 7:00 p.m.–7:30 p.m. Name That Anime Theme Song game and snacks
- 7:30 p.m.–8:00 p.m. Ramen-eating contest with chopsticks
- 8:00 p.m.–9:00 p.m. Murder by Candlelight game

NOTES

1. Interview with Chad Mairn, information services librarian and Innovation Lab manager at St. Petersburg College, conducted by the author, January 20, 2015.

2. Heidi MacDonald, "How to Throw a Comic Con at Your Library," *Publishers Weekly*, April 18, 2014, http://www.publishersweekly.com/pw/by-topic/industry-news/comics/article/61940-how-to-throw-a-comic-con-at-your-library.html.

3. Chad Mairn, "Organizing a Successful Comic Con at Your Library," *Slideshare*, March 2, 2015. http://www.slideshare.net/chadmairn/comic-con-45333394.

4. Ibid.

5. Interview with Carrie Rogers-Whitehead, senior librarian of teen services at the Salt Lake County Library, conducted by the author, January 26, 2015.

6. Spartanchef, "Japan's largest 'Cosplay Theme Park,' Haco Stadium Tokyo.One, Opens," *SG Cafe*, December 1, 2014, http://sgcafe.com/2014/12/japans-largest-cosplay-theme-park-haco-stadium-tokyo-one-opens/.

7. Interview with Carrie Rogers-Whitehead.

8. "NYCC Eastern Championships of Cosplay Rules," New York Comic Con, accessed April 23, 2015, http://www.newyorkcomiccon.com/Events/NYCC-Eastern-Championships-of-Cosplay/NYCC-Eastern-Championships-of-Cosplay-Rules/.

9. "San Diego Comic-Con International Masquerade—Contestant Information & Rules," San Diego Comic-Con International 2014, accessed April 23, 2015, http://www.comic-con.org/sites/default/files/forms/cci2014_masqrules_v1.pdf.

10. Interview with Brian Stephenson, brand marketing director; Justin Flores, content and talent coordinator; and Chris Malico, international content coordinator, all at ReedPop, conducted by the author, January 30, 2015.

11. Ibid.

12. "Anime Club Starter Kit," Anime Clubs Unite, accessed April 23, 2015, http://animeclubsunite.org/starter_kit/.

13. Andrea H. @Central and Peter B. @Dayton's Bluff, "How to Host an Anime Club," *In the Loop*, November 21, 2012, http://intheloopsppl.blogspot.com/2012/11/how-to-host-anime-club.html.

14. Calliope Woods, "Getting (and Keeping) Teens in Your Anime Club," *Cosplay, Comics, and Geek Culture in Libraries*, January 5, 2015, http://ccgclibraries.com/getting-and-keeping-teens-in-your-anime-club/.

15. Andrea H. @Central and Peter B. @Dayton's Bluff, "How to Host an Anime Club."

16. Interview with Heather Warren Smith, youth services librarian at ELANCO Library, conducted by the author, January 27, 2015.

17. "Anime Club Starter Kit."

18. Interview with Janet Hollingsworth, teen guide and 3-D printing guru at Anythink Brighton, and Jackie Kuusinen, branch manager/experience expert at Anythink Brighton, conducted by the author, March 13, 2015.

19. Ibid.

20. Ibid.

21. Ibid.

22. Svetlana Quindt, *The Book of Cosplay: Armor Making: With Worbla and Wonderflex* (Nuremberg, Germany: Author, 2014).

23. Ibid.

24. Svetlana Quindt, *The Book of Cosplay Painting: With Brushes and Acrylics* (Nuremberg, Germany: Author, 2014).

25. Svetlana Quindt in *Armor Painting*, April 15, 2015.

26. Dan Reeder, *Papier-Mâché Monsters: Turn Trinkets and Trash into Magnificent Monstrosities* (Layton, Utah: Gibbs Smith, 2009).

27. Ibid.

28. Thomas Glucksmann-Smith, "Cosplay Business Cards," *Shift East* (blog), May 2, 2013, http://www.shifteast.com/cosplay-business-cards/.

29. E. Arita and E. Corkill, "Fashion Fantasies Come to Life in Cosplay," *McClatchy—Tribune Business News*, March 9, 2008, retrieved from http://search.proquest.com/docview/465842654?accountid=130717.

30. Rachel Tackett, "The Lowdown on Japan's Cosplay Industry," *Rocket News 24*, May 16, 2013, http://en.rocketnews24.com/2013/05/16/the-lowdown-on-japans-cosplay-industry/.

31. Interview with Heather Warren Smith.

32. Lucas Siegel, "Marvel Announces *Black Panther, Captain Marvel, Inhumans, Avengers: Infinity War* Films, *Cap & Thor 3* Subtitles," *NewsaRama*, October 28, 2014, http://www.newsarama.com/22573-marvel-announces-black-panther-captain-marvel-inhumans-avengers-infinity-war-films-cap-thor-3-subtitles.html.

33. Marc Strom, "Marvel Studios Schedules New Release Dates for 4 Films," *Marvel Studios*, February 9, 2015, http://marvel.com/news/movies/24065/marvel_studios_schedules_new_release_dates_for_4_films.

34. Rob Keyes, "DC Movie Release Schedule Unveiled: *Wonder Woman & Justice League* in 2017," *ScreenRant*, October 21, 2014, http://screenrant.com/dc-movies-justice-league-wonder-woman-release-dates/.

35. "*Star Wars*," *Wikipedia*, accessed April 23, 2015. http://en.wikipedia.org/wiki/Star_Wars.

36. Tackett, "The Lowdown on Japan's Cosplay Industry."

7

Cosplay Issues, Tips, and Tricks

Cosplay, or costume play, is a fun and rewarding hobby with a rich community of people. Libraries can play a valuable role in that exciting community by providing services such as cosplay programming and events, integrating with local cosplay groups, and developing relevant collections. What else should you be aware of before implementing a cosplay program in your library? It may be helpful to have a bit of background about some of the issues and themes that are unique to the cosplay community so that when you are planning and hosting events, you are sensitive to these concerns.

CROSSPLAY: GENDER AND COSPLAY

A subset of cosplay, crossplay is less of an issue than a trend in the cosplay community. It is the practice of cosplaying a character of the opposite gender. The most common type of crossplay is female-to-male costuming; however, there are many examples of men cosplaying female characters. These gender-bending cosplays put a new spin on traditional characters such as female versions of the Joker, Link from *The Legend of Zelda*, Thor and Loki, Wolverine,[1] and even Doctor Who, as well as male versions of Sailor Moon, Wonder Woman, and Harley Quinn. Crossplay is about empowerment and the ability to dress as any type of character that you identify with,[2] regardless of gender, and is not in any way a statement on sexual orientation.[3] More information on this theme in cosplay can be found on the Crossplay.net discussion forums.

COSPLAY IS NOT CONSENT

Created to combat sexual harassment in the cosplay community, the "Cosplay is not consent" maxim has quickly become an accepted motto in the cosplay community. It refers to the verbal and physical sexual harassment experienced by (mainly female) cosplayers, including lewd and suggestive comments, stalking, inappropriate photography such as up-skirt photos, groping, and unwanted touching.[4]

The Geeks for CONsent (http://www.geeksforconsent.org) advocacy group, created by the female trio behind HollabackPHILLY, an anti–street harassment network, has been raising awareness about this important issue since 2013 through convention panels and booths spreading the "Cosplay ≠ CONsent" message. They also started an online petition that garnered 2,600 signatures and called for the San Diego Comic-Con organizers to create a formal antiharassment policy and an educational comic book. Another group, CosplayIsNotConsent.org, has accrued more than thirteen thousand likes on their Facebook page (https://www.facebook.com/CosplayIsNotConsent). In 2014, New York Comic Con showed its support for this important issue by creating an official antiharassment policy, which was prominently displayed at the October event. Con-goers were greeted with imposing signs[5] stating: "Cosplay is not consent. Keep your hands to yourself. If you would like to take a picture with or of another NYCC Fan, always ask first and respect that person's right to say no. When at NYCC, be respectful, be nice, be cool and be kind to each other."[6] To read NYCC's full harassment policy see http://www.newyorkcomiccon.com/About/Harassment-Policy.

RACE AND COSPLAY

Cosplay is an expression of fandom for a character, which is why many cosplayers will create costumes for characters outside of their own race. Many Westerners who cosplay anime characters take part in this practice,[7] as well as cosplayers portraying alien races from films such as *Avatar*. Race-bending in cosplay is generally accepted as long as costumes are respectful. But it is important to be aware that when cosplaying outside of your race, it is essential to be sensitive to elements of your costume that could be considered offensive. For example, it is never acceptable to use blackface or brownface when cosplaying, even if you are trying to be as authentic as possible. When the race is fictional, for example, the Na'vi race of Pandora (*Avatar*)[8] or Gamora from *Guardians of the Galaxy*, you can feel free to alter your skin tone to blue, green, and so on. Don't forget that cosplay is supposed to be fun. You should cosplay characters that you admire and identify with, regardless of race; just be considerate of others.

ACCESSIBILITY AND COSPLAY

Many comic book conventions provide accessibility services for attendees with special needs. Each convention page should have its own section discussing how these needs are met. San Diego Comic-Con leads the way by providing wheelchairs for loan, American Sign Language interpreters for deaf fans attending panels, special disabled seating, registration services, and reserved rest areas, as well as a dedicated Deaf and Disabled Services Team organizing these efforts.[9] There are also many fans with disabilities who have created some utterly ingenious costumes, including constructing Daleks and the TARDIS from *Doctor Who* around their wheelchairs, as well as the Iron Throne from Game of Thrones, and vehicles such as a TIE fighter and the Millennium Falcon from Star Wars, *TRON* vehicles, and a S.W.A.T. tank. Others portray characters who cannot walk, such as Professor Xavier from *X-Men* and the Little Mermaid. CosAbility—cosplay for those with disabilities, at https://www.facebook.com/CosAbility—is a Facebook group that provides tips for how to integrate your disability into your cosplay.

Misa on Wheels

https://www.facebook.com/MisaOnWheels
27,651 likes

Amanda Knightly, aka Misa on Wheels, is a well-known New England–based cosplayer who was born with a form of muscular dystrophy, which has left her partially paralyzed.[10] She attends many conventions in cosplay, spreading the message that "anyone can do anything they put their mind to and make their dreams come true!"[11] She provides inspiration to cosplayers with disabilities and those without through her photos with motivational quotes.

BODY IMAGE AND COSPLAY

The cosplay community is very sensitive to the issue of body shaming and most are quite outspoken about it, encouraging each other to cosplay whatever character they identify with, regardless of body size, shape, or type. Although the body-shaming issue is more of a concern for our culture as a whole, it does come into play in the cosplay community when negative or discouraging comments regarding costumes are made on social media or in person at conventions.[12] There are often panels at conventions discussing body image and cosplay, such as this one from the 2014 Big WOW Comicfest featuring Ivy Doomkitty, a regular speaker on the topic and an inspiration to many in the cosplay community:

"So They Say You Shouldn't Cosplay": http://tinyurl.com/poqympj.

Additionally, the Facebook page Cospositivity promotes an encouraging and positive cosplay community at https://www.facebook.com/Cospositivity.

COSPLAY AND SAFETY

The first and foremost concern in cosplay is safety. Many cosplayers are not prepared for long days at conventions and other costuming events and often do not consider planning for safety matters. This is an area where the library can take part and provide cosplayers with guidelines for their protection and well-being. Here are some safety tips that libraries can pass along to cosplayers for attending conventions:

- **Do not put your full name on your convention badge.** Always use either your first name alone or, better yet, your cosplay moniker so that you aren't providing any more personal and private information than absolutely necessary.[13]
- **Stay hydrated.** It's very easy to completely forget about drinking water while walking the convention floor for hours with your friends. There's a lot happening at these events, so it's important to stay hydrated while participating. Always arrive at the event with a bottle of water and schedule breaks throughout the day to keep yourself hydrated.[14]
- **Wear sunscreen.** Consider whether the event has an outdoor component or if your group will be planning group photo shoots in the parking lot or somewhere outside of the convention. If so, you'll want to wear or bring sunblock with you.[15]
- **Buddy up.** It's always best to use the buddy system at conventions and cosplay events. If you know that your friends are planning to go, ask to meet up with them when they arrive. That way you can look out for each other.[16]

- **Wear comfortable shoes.** Comic cons involve a *lot* of walking around, and cosplay photo shoot events involve a lot of standing around in one place either waiting or posing. It is important when you're planning your costumes to work around a pair of comfortable shoes, whether that means thinking about creating shoe or boot covers or investing in a new pair of flat walking shoes.[17]
- **Be sure to eat.** Just like staying hydrated, it is important to stay fed in order to keep up your energy. It is very easy to get caught up in all of the excitement and activities happening at conventions, and it is also very expensive to buy convention food, so it's important to have a plan for what you'll do for sustenance. If you'll be using the recommended buddy system, you can plan to go to a nearby establishment for lunch and then return to the con together.[18]
- **Plan a safe place for your belongings.** Costumes rarely come with pockets that are functional. Consider how you will carry your cash, ID, cell phone, and necessary makeup for your cosplay beforehand. You do not want to depend on needing to carry anything around in your hand, because you are likely at one point or another to put it down and leave it due to the fatigue and excitement of walking around the con. Boots make excellent holders for cell phones as well as cash and ID, as do geeky backpacks or small purses.[19]
- **Be aware of what's going on around you.** Always be aware of what's happening at conventions, and this is where the buddy system really helps out. In large crowds such as these, there are often people who are watching for the opportunity to take advantage of tired con-goers who leave their belongings unattended. Additionally, in a crowd of cosplayers, there are frequently spontaneous sword fights, impromptu light saber duels, and other such shenanigans. Stay well-fed and hydrated so that you can be mindful of all that's going on around you.
- **If it seems "off," don't do it.** Cosplayers meet all sorts of people and personalities at conventions. If someone offers you food or drinks or asks you to go somewhere with them and it seems weird, don't do it. It may be fine, but it's not worth the risk to be polite. Thank them and tell them that you are running late to meet your group.[20]
- **Be prepared for unwelcome photo requests.** Most requests for photos will be genuinely enjoyable for cosplayers, who have worked hard on their costumes and appreciate the attention that they get at the con. However, there are always those photographers who lack proper boundaries and will ask for more than they should. It's important for cosplayers to be aware that these requests may happen and have a plan to deal with them, such as a phrase or two that they have practiced beforehand. For example, photographers may ask you to strike a sexier pose than you are giving or may even ask you to turn around for a backside shot. To these you can simply reply "no thanks, these are my character's poses." Other frequent unwelcome photo requests at cons include vendors who ask cosplayers for photos while they hold up signs hawking their products/films/comics and those that want to hug, kiss, pick up, or otherwise get too familiar with cosplayers. In these cases, you may simply want to walk away. Again, having a friend or "buddy" along with you helps defuse many of these situations.[21]

Weapons Check

Every comic convention and cosplay event has a weapons policy. It is important to make cosplayers aware of what is allowed into most events and what is forbidden so that their prop weapons aren't confiscated. If the library will be hosting prop-making events at which cosplayers may be making their own replica weapons, this would be an excellent time to inform them about standard event policies. Most of these are clearly posted on event websites. Here is a standard cosplay weapons policy:

- Prop weapons that are made of light materials such as foam, cardboard, or wood are permissible. Prop firearms and other weapons must not be so realistic that they could be mistaken for actual weapons. Barrels of all prop firearms must have brightly colored caps in the barrels.
- No functional firearms (including air soft guns, paintball guns, etc.) or realistic-looking firearms that might be confused with functional firearms.
- No projectile weapons of any type, including water guns.
- No metal-bladed weapons, including swords.
- No real blunt weapons, such as nunchaku or brass knuckles.
- No hard prop weapons made of metal or fiberglass.
- No fireworks or explosives.[22]

TIPS AND TRICKS

What are some tips, tricks, and best practices that libraries can follow when it comes to integrating this exciting and fun hobby into their regular programming? Here are just a few words of advice gleaned from many helpful interviews and my own experiences as a cosplayer.

Offer those who can't afford to cosplay a way to join in the fun.

- Not everyone in your community is going to be able to afford to create cosplay costumes, but they may be interested in attending cosplay events such as workshops, fandom programs, and library lock-ins. You can make cosplaying at these events optional, as well as provide them with some inventive ideas for how to pull together a cosplay from items that they already own or can afford.[23] You might even offer cosplay consultations!
- Many of the projects provided in this book are aimed at cosplayers with a limited budget. By offering these types of events, libraries may be able to afford to purchase the required materials for participants who would like to learn these techniques, as well as offer them an affordable way to create their cosplays going forward

Educate yourself about major characters and fandoms.

- If you want to successfully integrate the types of services and programming discussed in this book, you will want to familiarize yourself with the major fandoms that your patrons are enthusiastic about so that you can develop appropriate programming. This will also help you highlight parts of the library's collection that may be relevant to particular genres, films, and series. See some of the suggested books in the resources at the end of the book to get you started.

Cosplay is about more than being judged.

- Cosplay contests are great fun for many cosplayers; however, most cosplayers create costumes to be a part of a community rather than to compete, so don't be surprised if some don't want to take part in a judged contest. There is an assumption that cosplayers dress in costume because they like attention, but many are shy. Those cosplayers enjoy paying homage to their favorite characters and spending time with their friends, but they don't want to be in the spotlight of an organized contest.

Provide your own tips and tricks for cosplayers.

• If there is an upcoming local convention or event that your community cosplayers are preparing for, why not provide them with a set of tips for safety and costume success such as last minute costume fixes, a list of essentials to bring with them to the con (e.g., fabric tape and safety pins), and maybe even some sewing tips.

Reach out to your community.

• Make connections and build relationships with local businesses such as comic book stores, gaming shops, and costume stores. Forge relationships with those in your local cosplay community—tips about doing this can be found in chapter 3, "Places to Go, People to See." And finally, reach out to your local maker community; many of them may be able to help out at 3-D printing events, or offer advice, feedback, and even troubleshooting help.

Don't feel like you need to know everything.

• You don't have to be a master artisan in order to offer workshops in materials such as in Worbla, EVA foam, 3-D printing, and so on. Of course, you want to be knowledgeable about how to work with each of them; however, you shouldn't feel that just because you aren't an engineer you shouldn't be hosting 3-D printing events. Yes, glitches may happen—but you can turn those glitches into teachable moments. You can also use all of the resources at your disposal in order to ensure a successful workshop which includes your local community. Don't be afraid to ask for help and for volunteers.

Remember to have fun!

• Don't forget that cosplay is a portmanteau of the words *costume* and *play*, with *play* being the key word. Cosplay is an incredibly fun, engaging, and fulfilling hobby; if you remember to have fun with it, your patrons will follow suit.

NOTES

1. Nate John, "Comic-Con 2014: A Crossplay Haven," *KPBS* (blog), August 1, 2014, http://www.kpbs.org/news/2014/aug/01/comic-con-2014-gender-bender-haven/.

2. Henry Hanks, "Costumed Fans Put a Gender Spin on Classic Characters," CNN, September 3, 2013, http://www.cnn.com/2013/09/03/living/cosplay-crossplay-dragoncon-irpt/.

3. Rachel Hui Ying Leng, "Gender, Sexuality, and Cosplay: A Case Study of Male-to-Female Crossplay," *The Phoenix Papers: First Edition*, April 2013, 103, http://nrs.harvard.edu/urn-3:HUL.InstRepos:13481274.

4. "Harassment Policy," New York Comic Con, accessed April 23, 2015, http://www.newyorkcomiccon.com/About/Harassment-Policy/.

5. Andrea Romano, "Cosplay Is Not Consent: The People Fighting Sexual Harassment at Comic Con," Mashable, October 14, 2014, http://mashable.com/2014/10/15/new-york-comic-con-harassment/.

6. "Harassment Policy."

7. Lady Saika, "Cosplay Questions: Race and Cosplay," *Lady Geek Girl and Friends* (blog), June 11, 2012, https://ladygeekgirl.wordpress.com/2012/06/11/cosplay-questions-race-and-cosplay/.

8. Victorianromantic, "Brownface in Cosplay: Why It Is Offensive to Some," *Korra Is Not Tan* (Tumblr blog), October 24, 2012, http://korraisnottan.tumblr.com/post/34258433334/brownface-in-cosplay-why-it-is-offensive-to-some.

9. "Deaf and Disabled Services," Comic-Con International: San Diego, accessed April 23, 2015, http://www.comic-con.org/cci/deaf-and-disabled-services.

10. Lauren Rae Orsini, "Misa on Wheels Rolls into Cosplay," *Daily Dot*, February 8, 2012, http://www.dailydot.com/entertainment/amanda-knightly-misa-on-wheels-cosplay/.

11. "Misa on Wheels," Facebook, accessed April 23, 2015, https://www.facebook.com/MisaOnWheels.

12. Joanna, "Cosplay, Race, and Fat-Shaming," *Geekalitarian* (blog), June 21, 2012, https://geekalitarian.wordpress.com/2012/06/21/cosplay-race-and-fat-shaming/.

13. "Safety Tips for Female Cosplayers," *Not Bad Cosplay* (Tumblr blog), December 19, 2012, http://notbadcosplay.tumblr.com/post/38354072020/safety-tips-for-female-cosplayers.

14. "Cosplay Health & Safety Tips!" WM Armory, September 14, 2014, http://www.wmarmory.com/?p=1193.

15. Ibid.

16. Ibid.

17. Ibid.

18. Ibid.

19. Ibid.

20. "Safety Tips for Female Cosplayers."

21. Emily Asher-Perrin, "How to Stay Safe When You Cosplay," Tor.com, November 1, 2013, http://www.tor.com/blogs/2013/11/how-to-stay-safe-when-you-cosplay.

22. "NYCC Eastern Championships of Cosplay Rules," New York Comic Con, accessed April 23, 2015, http://www.newyorkcomiccon.com/Events/NYCC-Eastern-Championships-of-Cosplay/NYCC-Eastern-Championships-of-Cosplay-Rules.

23. Interview with Kathleen Gruver, young adult librarian at the Burlington County Library System, conducted by the author, February 2, 2015.

Appendix A

Cosplay Event Activities

Here are the complete rules and project descriptions for the games mentioned in the text, Cosplay Iron Chef and Murder by Candlelight.

COSPLAY IRON CHEF

Contributed by Sarah Hodge-Wetherbe, library associate at Springfield City Library, Springfield, Massachusetts.

Materials Needed

- Three teams, five kids each (One kid is cosplay model, others are designers)
- Three judges
- One box of costume supplies
- This year our box included:
  o Clothes
  o Old curtains
  o A lace table cloth
  o Cardboard boxes
  o Cat ears on headband
  o Sunglasses
  o Permanent markers
  o Scissors
  o Duct tape
  o Two black domino masks
  o Three wigs (one long black, one long red, one short blue)
  o A pocket watch
  o Two hats (one a top hat, one a baseball cap)
  o Fourteen safety pins

I also had my tablet so that I could pull up pictures of characters. I used the timer function on my iPhone. Kids had ten minutes to put a costume together. The costume could be from any show, any character, or could be a generic geek category (steampunk, cyberpunk, etc.).

Rules were as follows:

- Only cardboard could be cut or written on/drawn on by permanent markers.
- Groups did not have to announce their character till the end of the ten minutes (giving them the flexibility to change their minds).
- Each group got one minute before the official time to quickly look through the box and see everything that was there.
- Judges rated on speed, accuracy to character/genre, and creativity in material use.

We awarded the winning team, and then the judges were able to pick two single players for special judges' choice awards for any reason they wanted. They chose one girl for modeling in character the best and one girl for a quick idea she had that saved the costume from being scrapped.

MURDER BY CANDLELIGHT

Contributed by Heather Warren Smith, youth services librarian, ELANCO Library, New Holland, Pennsylvania.

Best for ten or more players.

Preparation

- Cut squares of paper, one per player.
- Decide how many murderers you will need (usually one murderer for each ten players) and mark that number of papers with an "X."
- Place papers in a basket or bowl.

Objective

- If a victim—to find the murderer(s) while staying alive
- If a murderer—to kill all the victims (and other murderers, if applicable)

Rules

- Game is best played in a large area in the dark.
- Do not stay in groups—spread out!
- Keep moving around. If everyone just hides, the game will never end.
- A murder is committed by tapping the victim on the shoulder and the shoulder only, while stating, "You are dead." You must have both the physical and verbal actions!
- When someone is killed, he or she must scream loudly and fall down dead on the spot. This indicates to other players that a murderer is in the area.
- When you are dead, you stay dead. No walking around or telling living people who the murderer is!

- If you are still alive and think another player is the murderer, or if you witness a murder, you can accuse the murderer by stating, "You are the murderer." If that person is, in fact, the murderer, then they are dead (and must die appropriately). If they are not the murderer, the accuser is dead.

Game Play

- Have all players draw a paper. If they get a blank paper, they are a victim; if they get a paper with an "X," they are a murderer. Make sure that everyone knows how many murderers there are—this will reduce confusion at the end of the game.
- Send everyone out in the play area to roam around.
- Murderers kill people; victims try to stay alive.
- Game is over when there is only one person left alive. That's the winner! Turn the lights back on, pick new murderers, and start again.

Notes

They all cheat and they all hide. Mostly, dead people get bored and get up and move around (we call them zombies and have to remind them "no zombies!") If playing on more than one floor, we check continuously for inappropriate behavior. Library teens generally aren't the kind to go make out in the dark, but you never know.

Appendix B

Suppliers Directory

Worbla

- CosplaySupplies.com: http://www.cosplaysupplies.com
- The Engineer Guy: http://tinyurl.com/preol3s
- Local Retailers: http://www.worbla.com/?p=27
- Yaya Han: http://yayahan.bigcartel.com

Wonderflex

- CosplaySupplies.com: http://www.cosplaysupplies.com
- The Engineer Guy: http://tinyurl.com/k465md8
- Wonderflex World: http://www.wonderflexworld.com

EVA Foam

- Amazon: http://tinyurl.com/pr3k5s2
- Harbor Freight Tools: http://tinyurl.com/kbkd22a
- Home Depot: http://tinyurl.com/lv6fz54
- Walmart: http://tinyurl.com/o7sqjjj
- Sears: http://tinyurl.com/ku6bre2

Craft Foam

- Hobby Lobby: http://tinyurl.com/l29oerd
- Michaels: http://tinyurl.com/q4dfhob
- Walmart: http://tinyurl.com/oacforu

Commissions

- Anovos: http://www.anovos.com
- Beyond Creative Costumes!: https://www.facebook.com/pages/Beyond-Creative-Cos tumes/135833169787586
- Castle Corsetry: http://tinyurl.com/pyvv59c
- C. M. Prop Works (San Antonio): https://www.facebook.com/cosplay.props.needs
- Dadpool Cosplay and Props: https://www.facebook.com/DadpoolCosplay
- Etsy: https://www.etsy.com
- JJ Armory Inc.: https://www.facebook.com/jjarmoryinc
- Myratheon Cosplay: https://www.facebook.com/MyratheonCosplay
- Organic Armor: http://organicarmor.com
- Sonic Ascendancy Props (Black Hills): https://www.facebook.com/SonicAscendancyProps
- Sugar Smacks Design and Aesthetics: https://www.facebook.com/sugarsmacksdesign

Appendix C

Cosplayers Directory

COSPLAY GROUPS

- The 1701st Fleet: Star Trek Fandom: https://www.facebook.com/The1701stFleet
- 501st Legion: Vader's Fist: http://www.501st.com
- Alabama Ghostbusters: https://www.facebook.com/alabamaghostbusters
- Alternate Identities: https://www.facebook.com/pages/Alternate-Identities/10176263668 4388
- Austin Browncoats: http://www.austinbrowncoats.com
- California Browncoats: http://www.californiabrowncoats.org
- Empire Saber Guild: http://empiresaberguild.com
- The Ghostbusters of New Hampshire: https://www.facebook.com/GhostbustersofNew Hampshire
- Harry Potter Alliance: http://thehpalliance.org
- Heroes 4 Hire: http://www.theheroes4hire.com
- Indiana Ghostbusters: Jasper District: https://www.facebook.com/IN.GBJasper
- Real Tampa Bay Ghostbusters: http://tinyurl.com/lvjcg29
- The Rebel Legion: http://www.rebellegion.com
- Sacramento Ghostbusters: https://www.facebook.com/sacghostbusters
- Southeastern Browncoats: http://www.southeasternbrowncoats.com
- Umbrella Corporation Jacksonville (Home of the 219th Brain Surgeons): https://www .facebook.com/umbrellajacksonville

Librarian Cosplayers

Arkansas
Jean Besaw
Rogers Public Library

Connecticut
Miss Molly "SuperGirl" Virello
Southington Public Library and Museum
https://www.facebook.com/heroarmycosplay

Florida
Heidi Colom
Tampa-Hillsborough County Public Library
http://www.cosplaylab.com/cosplayers/detail.asp?memberid=128

Idaho
Marcy Timblin
East Bonner County Library
https://www.facebook.com/ebonnerlibrary

Kentucky
Clint Renfro
Fairdale Branch Library

Maine
Wacky Wardrobe Wednesday
McArthur Public Library
https://www.pinterest.com/anorwood0081/wacky-wardrobe-wednesday/

Massachusetts
Auntie Cosplay
Springfield City Library
https://www.facebook.com/ByTheBookCosplay

Emma Caywood
http://emmacaywood.weebly.com/cosplay-and-other-awesome-things.html

Michigan
Kristin LaLonde
Chippewa River District Library
https://kristinlalonde.wordpress.com/cosplay/

Missouri
Angela Schoemehl
Kirkwood Public Library

New York
Giallo Girl Cosplay
The New York Law Institute
https://www.facebook.com/giallogirl

North Carolina
Matthew Z. Wood
Durham County Library

Utah
missrelena
Washington County Utah Library System—Hurricane Branch
http://missrelena.diviantart.com

Washington
Bubbles (Powerpuff Girl)
Puyallup Public Library
http://facebook.com/rhonda.puntney

COSPLAYERS DIRECTORY

Note: This list is based on the user-submitted list created by Daniel Vasey titled "The Cosplayer Nation Directory."[1] It is available as a file in the Cosplayer Nation Facebook group located at http://tinyurl.com/msghz45.

Australia
Creed Photography: https://www.facebook.com/creedphotography
Dad's Cosplay Workbench: https://www.facebook.com/dadscosplayworkbench
Julian Gemmell: https://www.facebook.com/julian.gemmell
Knitemaya: https://www.facebook.com/knitemaya
Shi Tenshi Cosplay: https://www.facebook.com/ShiTenshiCosplay

Austria
Bella-hime: https://www.facebook.com/adaira.cosplay

Bangladesh
BD Cosplayers: https://www.facebook.com/bdcosplayers
Big Red—Predator: https://www.facebook.com/yautjared
CatLady Cosplays: https://www.facebook.com/CatLadyCosplays
Cosplay.BD: https://www.facebook.com/cosplay.bd

Barbados
Trident Cosplay: https://www.facebook.com/TridentCosplay

Brazil
Eva Cosmaker: https://www.facebook.com/evacosmaker.1

Canada

New Brunswick
Shapeshifters Alley INC: https://www.facebook.com/pages/Shapeshifters-Alley-INC/1506581786244975

Hamilton, Ontario
Allure Cosplay: https://www.facebook.com/pages/Allure-Cosplay/943130679050189

Windsor, Ontario
  Star Lord Cosplay: https://www.facebook.com/starlordthelegendaryoutlaw

Toronto, Ontario
  Agent Elle Cosplay: https://www.facebook.com/agentellecosplayarts
  Lina Chu's Cosplay/Modelling: https://www.facebook.com/pages/Lina-Chu/130621363
    769840
  Mama Toph Cosplay: https://www.facebook.com/mamatophcosplay
  Pinkiebel Design: https://www.facebook.com/pinkiebelcostumes
  Summer Edwards Cosplay/Modeling/Photography: https://www.facebook.com/Summer
    VioletEdwards
  Yukihime Cosplay: https://www.facebook.com/pages/Yukihime-Cosplay/501446233306
    959

Sherbrooke, Quebec
  Marie Ventress Cosplay: https://www.facebook.com/pages/Marie-Ventress-Cosplay/2494
    54611923649

Chile
  Emina Cosplay: https://www.facebook.com/eminacosplay
  Hakurei Cosplay: https://www.facebook.com/HakureiCos

Colombia
  Arual ebiru: https://www.facebook.com/ARUAL.EBIRU.S

Cyprus
  Margarita Kotsoni: https://mdragonheartlove.deviantart.com

France
  Aure Ore: https://www.facebook.com/aure.ore
  Shae Underscore: https://www.facebook.com/shae.underscore
  Sylyne Cosplay: https://www.facebook.com/SylyneCosplay

Germany
  JenNyan: https://www.facebook.com/iJenNyan
  Kamui Cosplay: http://www.kamuicosplay.com

Ireland
  Big Red: Predator: https://www.facebook.com/yautjared
  Cairdiúil: https://www.facebook.com/cairduels
  Cosplay Ireland: https://www.facebook.com/pages/Cosplay-Ireland/208061702570277

Japan
  Fenix D'Joan: https://www.facebook.com/FenixD.Joan

Kuwait
  Q8 Cosplayers! (Kuwait): https://www.facebook.com/q8cosplayers

New Zealand
Sin Cosplay: https://www.facebook.com/xlordsinx

Pakistan
Faizan Mughal—Pakistani Cosplayer: https://www.facebook.com/fmcosplays
Pakistani Cosplayers: https://www.facebook.com/pak.cosplayers

Philippines
Alodia Gosiengfiao: https://www.facebook.com/AlodiaGosiengfiao
R.A.W: https://www.facebook.com/realawesomeworkz

Russia
Kain&Nathan Li cosplay: https://www.facebook.com/kainnathanli
Sunji cosplay: https://www.facebook.com/SunjiCosplay

South Africa
Neko Cosplay RU: https://www.facebook.com/ruNekoCosplay

Spain
Ilustrastudios (Elche): https://www.facebook.com/ilustrastudios1
Kiddo Cosplay: https://www.facebook.com/BeatrizGarciaCosplay
Prnze: https://www.facebook.com/PrnzeTitan
Revolver Cosplay & Reenactment (Barcelona): https://www.facebook.com/RevolverCR

United Kingdom
Sisko the Protagonist Cosplay: https://www.facebook.com/SiskoTheProtagonistCosplay
ThePrimeAvenger: https://www.facebook.com/theprimeavenger

United States of America
Alabama

Crafty Christine: https://www.facebook.com/craftychristine1
Ghoultastic Monsters (Hartselle): https://www.facebook.com/pages/Ghoultastic-Monsters/1706821639544673
iHunter: Cosplayer (Holly Pond/Cullman): https://www.facebook.com/ihunterofficial
War Room Cosplay (Gadsden): https://www.facebook.com/warroomcosplay
Wonder Woman of North Alabama (North Alabama): https://www.facebook.com/Wonderwomanofnorthalabama

Alaska
Masked Sashimi Kids: https://www.facebook.com/sashimikamen/

Arizona
Juno Cosplay: https://www.facebook.com/junosomething
Kitteninstrings Cosplay: https://www.facebook.com/kitteninstringscosplay
Tucson Spider-Girl: https://www.facebook.com/TucsonSpiderGirl

Arkansas

2 Nerds in Love: https://www.facebook.com/ellibunneh

California

Alexander Rae: https://www.facebook.com/Alexrae64

Aurora Kaganshiko: https://www.facebook.com/pages/Aurora-Kaganshiko/130950230334273

Celeste Orchid: https://www.facebook.com/My.Celeste.Orchid

Chibi Bubble Ninja: https://www.facebook.com/Chibibubbleninja

Chibi Bubble Ninja's Sewing & Kigurumi Cafe: https://www.facebook.com/chibibubbleninjassewingcafe

DataFist: https://www.facebook.com/DataFist

Erin DeBorba Cosplay: https://www.facebook.com/erindeborba91

GamerGirl: https://www.facebook.com/Gamer.Girl.AX

The Geeky Gamer Girl: https://www.facebook.com/TheGeekyGamerGirl

Ivy Doomkitty: https://www.facebook.com/ivydoomkittyivy

Kelton.: https://www.facebook.com/kerukeruuu

Lady Pepper, The Madame of Mischief: https://www.facebook.com/LadyPepperCosplayer

Lionel Lum: https://www.facebook.com/lionel.lum.5

Mai Chan: https://www.facebook.com/MaiyukiChan

Maridah: https://www.facebook.com/MaridahCosplay

Nicole Marie Jean: https://www.facebook.com/NicoleMarieJeanPage

Usagi Chokorēto: https://www.facebook.com/bunnyslave4u

Vampy: https://www.facebook.com/VAMPYBITME

Warflight Wrong Studios: https://warflight.darkfolio.com/

Colorado

Aurora Hail Frost Cosplay: https://www.facebook.com/AurorahailfrostCosplay

Convention TaskForce: https://www.facebook.com/groups/ConventionTaskForce

Drunken Bobs Creations: https://www.facebook.com/DrunkenBobsCreations

Evil Mech Meru Cosplay: https://www.facebook.com/EvilMechMeruCosplay

Xiled Cosplays: https://www.facebook.com/XiledCosplays

Connecticut

Afro-Pic: https://www.facebook.com/AfroPicProductions

Azumii Cosplay: https://www.facebook.com/AzumiiCosplay

Chibi Mai Cosplay: https://www.facebook.com/ChibiMaiCosplay

Essie Cosplay: https://www.facebook.com/essiecosplay

Jenna Priz: https://www.facebook.com/jennapriz

Justin Anderson: https://www.facebook.com/D00mS0ng

Kitteninstrings Cosplay: https://www.facebook.com/kitteninstringscosplay

Secret Cosplayer: https://www.facebook.com/SecretCosplayer

D.C.

America's Greatest Otaku Chris Wanamaker: https://www.facebook.com/AmericasGreatestOtakuChrisWanamaker

AnnihilAsian KozPlay: https://www.facebook.com/AnnihilAsian.KozPlay

Momo Cosplay and Photography: https://www.facebook.com/321momo

Tony R Ray: https://www.facebook.com/EverybodyLovesTonyRay

Zazie Cosplay: https://www.facebook.com/zaziecosplay

Delaware

   Nitsuku Cosplay: https://www.facebook.com/nitsukucosplayfan

Florida

   A to Z Cosplay (Orlando): https://www.facebook.com/AtoZCosplay

   B-Dancer Cosplay: https://www.facebook.com/Bdancercosplay

   Chameleon Cosplay: https://www.facebook.com/pages/Chameleon-Cosplay/261707297
      368851

   Cosplay Snapped: https://www.facebook.com/CosplaySnapped

   D99Inc: https://www.facebook.com/D99INc

   Diogenia Cosplay: https://www.facebook.com/diogeniacosplay

   Ginomai Films Limited (New Port Richey): https://www.facebook.com/ginomaifilms

   Hanabi Flare (花火フレア): https://facebook.com/hanabiflare

   Juliet Audrey Winchester: https://www.facebook.com/JulietAudreyWinchester

   Kimberly Moore: https://www.facebook.com/KimberlyMooreOfficial

   Lady Luminous Cosplay: https://www.facebook.com/LadyLuminousCosplay

   Leaping Lizard Cosplay: https://www.facebook.com/leapinglizardcosplay

   MakeupSiren: https://www.facebook.com/Makeupsirencom

   Merrypranxter: https://www.facebook.com/merrypranxter

   Mowseler: https://www.facebook.com/mowseler

   Princess Porcelain: https://www.facebook.com/PrincessPorcelain

   Shino Usagi Cosplay: https://www.facebook.com/ShinoUsagiCosplay

   Tails of the Blade: https://www.facebook.com/TailsoftheBlade

   There Is No Spoon Productions: https://www.facebook.com/TINSProductions

Georgia

   Asch Spectre: https://www.facebook.com/aschspectre

   Crochet Cosplay: https://www.facebook.com/MillinCosplay

   DH Cosplay (Albany): https://www.facebook.com/DHcosplay

   Kitty's Cake: https://www.facebook.com/Kittycakecosplay

   Lady Lee Cosplay: https://www.facebook.com/LadyLeeCosplay

   Merrypranxter: https://www.facebook.com/merrypranxter

   Monika Lee: https://www.facebook.com/London2191Cosplay

   Yaya Han: https://www.facebook.com/yayacosplay

   Yuki Kuma: https://www.facebook.com/ShayLalaMina

Hawaii

Idaho

Illinois

   Ashurii Yuki: https://www.facebook.com/AshuriiYuki

   Chicago Loki: https://www.facebook.com/chicagoloki

   Fanservice Renji: https://www.facebook.com/pages/FanService-Renji/118427704886344

   The wauconda Spiderman: https://www.facebook.com/pages/The-wauconda-Spiderman/
      322874517915693

Indiana

   Final Fantasy Cosplayer—Julie: https://www.facebook.com/finalfantasycosplayjulie

   LadyDragon Cosplay Creations (Cass County): https://www.facebook.com/ladydragoncre-
      ations

Momo Kurumi Cosplay: https://www.facebook.com/MomoKurumiCosplay

Panda2Chu: https://www.facebook.com/panda2chu

Iowa

Kansas

Pyramid Head the Cosplayer: https://www.facebook.com/pages/Pyramid-Head-the-Co-splayer/476337675721831

Sophii Cosplay: https://www.facebook.com/UltraGirlsCosplay

Sparqy Cosplay: https://www.facebook.com/sparqycosplay

Kentucky

Chaos Creations Cosplay: https://www.facebook.com/chaos.creations.cosplay

Louisiana

Miss Marquin: https://www.facebook.com/MissMarquin

Star's Cosplays: https://www.facebook.com/pages/Stars-Cosplays/768011763245281

Maine

Kitteninstrings Cosplay: https://www.facebook.com/kitteninstringscosplay

Maryland

Envy Cosplay: https://www.facebook.com/EnvyCosplay

Laurie Glimmer: https://www.facebook.com/LaurieGlimmer

Masauku1: https://www.facebook.com/Masauku1

StevePool Cosplay: https://www.facebook.com/deadpoolmeetsnightwing

Studio Eingana: https://www.Facebook.com/StudioEingana

Massachusetts

AE Cosplay: https://www.facebook.com/AEcosplay

ATK PWR: https://www.facebook.com/pages/ATK-PWR/241068599396848

Boston's Deadpool: https://www.facebook.com/bostonsdeadpool

Bunny Moon Cosplay: https://www.facebook.com/BunnyMoonCosplay

DaiyaBolic: https://www.facebook.com/DiabolicKei

Danny the Pipes: https://www.facebook.com/pages/Danny-The-Pipes/1444854522394398

Gaius Iulius Tabernarius: https://www.facebook.com/GaiusIuliusTabernarius

Kokuujin: https://www.facebook.com/Kokuujin

Kuma Works: https://www.facebook.com/KumaWorks

La Latina Otaku Cosplay: https://www.facebook.com/pages/La-Latina-Otaku-Cosplay/1458161017741572

Man 0f Steel: https://www.facebook.com/supermankallosel

Misa on Wheels: https://www.facebook.com/MisaOnWheels

Phoenix Cosplay: https://www.facebook.com/pages/Phoenix-Cosplay/338483959656443

Reverie Cosplay: https://www.facebook.com/ReverieCosplay

Solo Grayson: https://www.facebook.com/SoloGrayson

Squeaky Hime Cosplay: https://www.facebook.com/pages/Squeaky-Hime-Cosplay/1494710024093582

Sterling Arts & Cosplay: https://www.facebook.com/Sterlingartscosplay

The Matrix Cosplay and Photography: https://www.facebook.com/thematrixcosplay

Toku-Breaker Cosplay: https://www.facebook.com/pages/Toku-Breaker-Cosplay/329138
030544706

Volkodav Cosplay: https://www.facebook.com/VolkodavCosplay

Michigan

Kira Elric/KamuiYamato: https://www.facebook.com/pages/Kira-Elric-KamuiYamato/19
5382153822121

Power-Up Cosplays: https://www.facebook.com/pages/Power-Up-Cosplays/3972858137
54440

Minnesota

Larina Cosplay: https://www.facebook.com/pages/Larina/173250326069915

Nyla Lee: https://www.facebook.com/NylaCosplay

Mississippi

Lellenshmellen Cosplay: https://www.facebook.com/lellenshmellencosplay

Yunarashi: https://www.facebook.com/Geek.Dropbox

Missouri

Dr. Crossplay: https://www.facebook.com/doctorcrossplay

Waterlily Cosplay: https://www.facebook.com/pages/Waterlily-Cosplay/410997175
60443

Rachelle Yuitza: https://www.facebook.com/rachelleyuitza

Blundergirl Whovian: https://www.facebook.com/blundergirl.whovian

Montana

Nebraska

Anastasia August: https://www.facebook.com/anastasiaaugusts

Commando Cosplay.: https://www.facebook.com/pages/Commando-Cosplay/77444891
9275876

Katie Otten: http://www.facebook.com/katieotten13

Nickie Bonar: https://www.facebook.com/The.Twisted.Belle

Nevada

Jessica Nigri: https://www.facebook.com/OfficialJessicaNigri

New Hampshire

Allie Cosplays: https://www.facebook.com/alliecosplays

Cosplay Chowie: https://www.facebook.com/chowie4love

New Jersey

Chibi Inu Tsuzuki Cosplay: https://www.facebook.com/ChibiInuTsuzukiCosplay

Dokudel: https://www.facebook.com/dokudelcosplay

EyesofNation: https://www.facebook.com/NationsCosplay

Gia Sanrio: https://www.facebook.com/GiaSanrio

Lily Stitches: https://www.facebook.com/lilystitches

Mixedupcosplay: https://www.facebook.com/pages/Mixedupcosplay/1394603304095717

Rockstar Cosplay: https://www.facebook.com/rocknrollcosplay

Seibatooth Cosplay: https://www.facebook.com/seibatoothcosplay

New Mexico
  Ashe Kai: https://www.facebook.com/ashekaiofficial
  Back to One Props Cosplay: https://www.facebook.com/BackToOneProps
  The Keeper Thief Cosplay: https://www.facebook.com/TheKeeperThiefCosplay

New York City
  8 Bit Bakeshop: https://www.facebook.com/8bitbakeshop
  Akira93 Cosplay: https://www.facebook.com/pages/Akira93-Cosplay/318707614935812
  Amy-Lee Cosplay: https://www.facebook.com/AmyLeeCosplay
  Andrew Arkham Cosplay: https://www.facebook.com/AndrewArkhamCosplay
  Anthony Murray: https://www.facebook.com/Pikaman206
  Ani-Mia: https://www.facebook.com/Ani.Mia.Cosplay
  Chameleon Cosplay: https://www.facebook.com/LolaChameleon
  Charles Battersby: https://www.facebook.com/charles.battersby.9
  Chris Smith: https://www.facebook.com/chris.nyr
  Christopher Troy: https://www.facebook.com/christopher.troy.75
  Crystal Gem: https://www.facebook.com/CrystalsMangaCafe
  Crystalninastar: https://www.facebook.com/Crystalninastar
  Dark Elven/Neko Hentaigirl: https://www.facebook.com/DarkElvenNekoHentaigirl
  Darlena Marie Cosplays: https://www.facebook.com/DarlenaMarieCosplays
  Dave Mal: https://instagram.com/fallnmerc
  Delta Major: https://www.facebook.com/DeltaMajor
  ElectroCosplay: https://www.facebook.com/Electrocosplay
  Endymion Mageto: https://www.facebook.com/endymageto
  Frankie Koelle: https://www.facebook.com/frankie.koelle
  Giallo Girl Cosplay: https://www.facebook.com/giallogirl
  Inochii/Nerdy Lolita: https://www.facebook.com/Inochii
  It's Showtime, PeachyMomo: https://www.facebook.com/showtime.peachymomo
  Joanna Mari Cosplay: https://www.facebook.com/joannamaricosplay
  Keith Grillman: https://www.facebook.com/keith.grillman
  Kenny Kosplay: https://www.facebook.com/pages/Kenny-Kosplay/275315015819855
  Koneko Your Average Nerd: https://www.facebook.com/KonekoYourAverageNerd
  Lilith Oya: https://www.facebook.com/LilithOya
  Margarita Kotsoni: https://mdragonheartlove.deviantart.com
  Matthew Fasanaro: https://www.facebook.com/mattty101
  Miggy Jagger: https://www.facebook.com/MiggyJagger
  Mika M. Cosplay: https://www.facebook.com/mikamcosplay
  Mina Monet: https://www.facebook.com/pages/Mina-Monet/525501697538334
  Miss Napalm Cosplay: https://www.facebook.com/MissNapalmCosplay
  Nathan Gonzalez Cosplay: https://www.facebook.com/OfficialNathanGonzalez
  Negative Stacey: https://www.facebook.com/NegativeStacey
  Nox D Martinez: https://www.facebook.com/NoxCosplay
  OnyxGlow Cosplay: https://www.facebook.com/OnyxGlowCosplay
  Raymundo Aizen Grayson: https://www.facebook.com/RaymundoHeroNYC
  Saikai: https://www.facebook.com/SaikaiNoChiToBara
  Saraphina Wall: https://instagram.com/saraphina_clare
  Sheena Rodriguez: https://www.facebook.com/Rodriguez.Sheena

Siryn: https://www.facebook.com/InoElricArtisticSoul
Spectra Marvelous: https://www.facebook.com/Spectra.Marvelous
Stella Chuu: https://www.facebook.com/stellachuuuuu
Succubus Cosplay (Avacyn & ZeldaLilly): https://www.facebook.com/SuccubusCosplay
The Fan's P.O.V.: https://www.facebook.com/thefanspov
Ukihime Cosplay: http://instagy.com/user/ukihime_cosplay
Vaughn Delvalle Jr.: https://www.facebook.com/vaughn.j.delvalle
Visored Cosplay: https://www.facebook.com/VisoredCosplay

North Carolina

AislinOfDreams (Durham): http://aislinofdreams.deviantart.com/
Bada Boom Cosplay (Carrboro): https://www.facebook.com/BadaBoomCosplay
Blue Eyed Sisters (Fayetteville): https://www.facebook.com/BlueEyedSisters
Chancellor D Cosplay (Durham): https://www.facebook.com/chancellordcosplay
Charlie Rocket Cosplay (Raleigh): https://www.facebook.com/Charrocket
Claudia Vainglory (Raleigh): https://www.facebook.com/claudia.vainglory
Fushichō Cosplay (Apex/Durham): https://www.facebook.com/FushichoCosplay
Jackie Craft Cosplay: https://www.facebook.com/JackieCraftss
Kelton: https://www.facebook.com/kerukeruuu
Luna Vistara (Concord): https://www.facebook.com/LunaVistara
Misa Marie: https://www.facebook.com/MisaMarieCosplay
Miss Faye's Cosplay Closet: Supply: https://www.facebook.com/miss.faye.cosplay
OkWookiee Cosplay (Boone & Chapel Hill): https://www.facebook.com/okwookiecosplay
Stormy Blayze Cosplay (Wilmington): https://www.facebook.com/KyraBlayzeCosplay

North Dakota

Ohio

Akida Oh Aki Cosplay: https://www.facebook.com/AkidaOhAki
Amanda Leigh Cosplay: https://www.facebook.com/cosplayamanda
Knightmage: https://www.facebook.com/knightmage1
Nova Blackblood Cosplay: https://www.facebook.com/NovaBlackbloodCosplay
Reiko The Aristocrat: https://www.facebook.com/ReikoTheAristocrat
The Costume Kings: https://www.facebook.com/costumekings
Zaelyx Cosplay: https://www.facebook.com/ZaelyxCosplay

Oklahoma

Lieu Lu: https://www.facebook.com/LieuLuChan

Oregon

Pennsylvania

Captain Kyle: https://www.facebook.com/capkyle
Christine's Cosplay: https://www.facebook.com/pages/Christines-Cosplay/172423129628390
Emily Smith Photography: https://www.facebook.com/emilysmithphoto
Hurricane Kitten: https://www.facebook.com/HurricaneKittenCosplay
Lamia Creations: https://www.facebook.com/LamiaCreations
Lissie Rose Cosplay and Design: https://www.facebook.com/lissierosedesign

Nova Blackblood Cosplay: https://www.facebook.com/NovaBlackbloodCosplay
Res1ka Cosplay: https://www.facebook.com/Res1ka
Yama-chan Cosplay: https://www.facebook.com/ChristineCosplay

Puerto Rico
Daisy Ann Cosplay: https://www.facebook.com/DaisyAnnCosplay

Rhode Island

South Carolina
Beagle K Cosplay: https://www.facebook.com/BeagleKCosplay
Bur Loire: https://www.facebook.com/burloirecosplay
Cosplay and Warpaint: https://www.facebook.com/CosplayandWarpaintawesomeness
Magnolia Q Cosplay and Art: https://www.facebook.com/MagnoliaQcosplay
Mira Scarlet Cosplay: https://www.facebook.com/mirascarletcosplay
Takumi Cosplay: https://www.facebook.com/takumicosplay
Thel Phenom Cosplay: https://www.facebook.com/ThelPhenomCosplay
Tiffany Dawn Cosplay: https://www.facebook.com/tiffanydawncosplay
Tiffany Diaz Cosplay: https://www.facebook.com/TiffanyDiazCosplay

South Dakota
Starburst Cosplay (Black Hills): https://www.facebook.com/SBCosplay

Tennessee
Vedetta Marie (Chattanooga): https://www.facebook.com/VedettaMarie

Texas
BeFearless Cosplay: https://www.facebook.com/BeFearlessCosplay
Black Sheep Cosplay: https://www.facebook.com/blacksheepcos
BlackSix57: https://www.facebook.com/Blacksix57
C.M. Cosplay (San Antonio): https://www.facebook.com/CMM.cosplay
Camelot Cosplay: https://www.facebook.com/camelotcosplay
Cool By Proxy Productions (Tori McKenna & Josh Phelan): https://www.facebook.com/CoolByProxyProductions
DugFinn: https://www.facebook.com/dugfinncosplay
Heaven Cosplay: https://www.facebook.com/heavencosplay
Holly Gloha: https://www.facebook.com/Gloha.h
Jennlee Cosplay: https://www.facebook.com/Jennleescosplay
Jinxie: https://www.facebook.com/jinxiejem
Kappa Lizzy, Brain Tumor Survivor: https://www.facebook.com/KappaLizzy
Le'vanmarie Model/Dancer/Cosplayer (San Antonio): https://www.facebook.com/levanmariephb
MagicalMe Cosplay: https://www.facebook.com/MagicalMeCosplay
Mineralblu Photography: https://www.facebook.com/mineralblu
Qubit Cosplay: https://www.facebook.com/qubitcosplay
That Nerdy Cosplay Couple: https://www.facebook.com/thatnerdycosplaycouple
Woody and Shay Cosplay: https://www.facebook.com/woodyandshaycosplay

Utah
GeekGirls Corp: https://www.facebook.com/geekgirlscorp
Ronan Angelos: https://www.facebook.com/ronan.angelos

Vermont

Virginia

 AnnihilAsian KozPlay: https://www.facebook.com/AnnihilAsian.KozPlay
 Bobby Thompson: https://www.facebook.com/bobby.thompson.585112
 DanaBelle Cosplay: https://www.facebook.com/missdanabelle
 Half Way Cosplay: https://www.facebook.com/Halfwaycosplay
 Jordymassacre Cosplay: https://www.facebook.com/JordymassacreCosplay
 Kijai9Y0: https://www.facebook.com/Kijai9Y0Official
 NekoNerd: https://www.facebook.com/NekoDragonNerd
 PhantomHoodie: https://www.facebook.com/pages/PhantomHoodie/748425711852194
 Siegfried Cosplay: https://www.facebook.com/SiegfriedCosplay
 Striking Cosplay: http://www.facebook.com/strikingcosplay
 TifaIA Cosplay: https://www.facebook.com/TifaIACosplay
 Tiny Kitten Cosplay: https://www.facebook.com/tinykittencosplay

Washington

 Abi Sue Cosplay: https://www.facebook.com/AbiSueCosplay
 Adventures with Mala: https://www.facebook.com/AdventureswithMala
 Jerikandra Cosplay: https://www.facebook.com/jerikandracosplay
 Riri (リリ): https://www.facebook.com/RIRI.Cosplay
 Shroomu: https://www.facebook.com/ShroomuCosplay
 Vorel Darastrix: https://www.faccbook.com/voreldarastrixcosplay
 Zelda, Realized: https://www.facebook.com/ZeldaRealized

West Virginia

 Kaos Cosplays: https://www.facebook.com/KaosCosplays
 Raynebow Vomit Cosplays: https://www.facebook.com/RaynebowVomitCosplays

Wisconsin

 Armageddon Cosplay: https://www.facebook.com/pages/Armageddon-Cosplay/2090557
  95828679
 CC Cosplay Studios: https://www.facebook.com/CCCosplayStudios
 DarkQlue Cosplay (Qlue): https://www.faccbook.com/darkqlue

Wyoming

 Beagle K Cosplay: https://www.facebook.com/BeagleKCosplay
 Reverie Cosplay: https://www.facebook.com/ReverieCosplay
 Sunji cosplay: https://www.facebook.com/SunjiCosplay

NOTE

 1. Daniel Vasey, "The Cosplayer Nation Directory," Cosplayer Nation, accessed April 28, 2015, http://tinyurl.com/msghz45. (Must be a member of the Cosplayer Nation group to view.)

Appendix D

Photographers Directory

Note: This list is based on the user-submitted list created by Philip Ng, "Cosplay Photographers,"[1] located here: http://goo.gl/C1IVhQ.

Alabama
    Chris Auditore Photography (Huntsville, Fayetteville, Tullahoma): https://www.facebook.com/Chrisauditorephotography/

California
    Caperture Photography: https://www.facebook.com/CaperturePhotography
    Themed Shots: https://www.facebook.com/themedshots
    Wamser Photography: https://www.facebook.com/wamserphotography

Connecticut
    Afro-Pic Productions: https://www.facebook.com/AfroPicProductions
    Calico Jackson Photography: https://www.facebook.com/CalicoJacksonPhotography
    Jarzabek Photography: https://www.facebook.com/jarzabekphotography

Florida
    BAM Photography: https://www.facebook.com/BAMCosplayPhotography
    Cosplay Snapped: https://www.facebook.com/CosplaySnapped
    Gapple Photos: https://www.facebook.com/GapplePhotos
    KAS Photography: http://kasphotography.zenfolio.com/

Georgia
    Ginger Lamb Photography: https://www.facebook.com/gingerlambphotography
    Marcus Taylor Photography: https://www.facebook.com/marcustaylorphotography

Illinois
    Eddie B Photos: https://www.facebook.com/EddieBPhotos
    Ronald Ladao, Freelance Photographer: https://www.facebook.com/rladaophotos

Indiana
    Burch Roots Studio: https://www.facebook.com/burchrootsstudio

TheMOX: https://www.flickr.com/photos/20790907@N06/sets
Neitling Photography: https://www.facebook.com/NeitlingPhotography

Maine

JtPetrin Photography: https://www.facebook.com/JtPetrinPhotography

Maryland

Coolsteel27 Photography: https://www.facebook.com/Coolsteel27
M. B. Photography: https://www.facebook.com/mbcosplayphoto
Murritsmarra Photography: https://www.facebook.com/Murritsmarra
SF Design: https://www.facebook.com/SFDesign21
Splashing Lights Photography: https://www.facebook.com/TwoCamsSnaps

Massachusetts

Dave Yang Photography: https://www.facebook.com/DaveYangPhotography
John Chea Photography: https://www.facebook.com/johncheaphotography
Kaze To Mizu Photography: https://www.facebook.com/kazetomizuphotography
Lazzaro Studios: https://www.facebook.com/LazzaroStudios
Marmaladeskys Photography: https://www.facebook.com/Marmaladeskysgirl45Photography
Punto De Aries/Phos-GraphΦs: https://www.facebook.com/punto.aries.phos.graphos
Vander Photography: https://www.facebook.com/VanderPhotography

Michigan

Errant Knight Photography: http://www.errantknightphotography.com
Happy Pause Photography: https://www.facebook.com/HappyPausePhoto
Littlecats Photography: https://www.facebook.com/littlecatsphoto

New Jersey

Cozpho Photography: https://www.facebook.com/Cozpho
Future Photography By M3: https://www.facebook.com/FuturePhotographybyM3
HSL Photography: https://www.facebook.com/HslPhotography
Jacob Gonzalez: http://www.mochipix.com
J. Snipe Photography: https://www.facebook.com/JSnipePhotography
KG Photography: https://www.facebook.com/KGcosplayphoto
Luciano Alicea: http://www.neociano.com
PWNstar Cosplay and Photography: https://www.facebook.com/iampwnstar

New York

A. G. Vask: https://www.facebook.com/A.G.Vask
Alchemist Photography: https://www.facebook.com/alchemist.fotos
Alex Valderana Photography: https://www.facebook.com/ValderanaPhotos
BAS Photography and Design: https://www.facebook.com/basphotographydesign
Bryan Lee Cruz Photography: https://www.facebook.com/blcruzphoto
Carlos A. Smith Photography: https://www.facebook.com/carlos.a.smith.7
ConPics: https://www.facebook.com/conpics
Darren Hall: https://www.flickr.com/photos/30376848@N06
D. Brooks Photos82: https://www.facebook.com/DBrooksPhoto82
Freeze Frame Foto: https://www.facebook.com/freezeframenyc
GeekedPhotography: https://www.facebook.com/geekedphotos

Jason Chau Photography: https://www.facebook.com/JasonChauPhotography
Jason Laboy: http://www.jasonlaboyphotography.com
Knightmare6: https://www.facebook.com/knightmare6photo
Kuchizuke Photography: https://www.facebook.com/kuchizukephotos
Lazy Cat Cosplay and Photography: https://www.facebook.com/lazycatcosplay
Neeko Cosplay and Photography: https://www.facebook.com/neekocosplay
PM Photography: https://www.facebook.com/PMPhotographyNYC
Robert Velasco Photography: http://robertvelasco.com
Ron Gejon Photography: https://www.facebook.com/RonGejonPhotography
Rudi B Photography: https://www.facebook.com/rudibphotography
Soul-Drive Photography: https://www.facebook.com/souldrivephotography
That DJ Ranma S Guy: https://www.facebook.com/IAMDJRanmaS
Vicious Victor's Photography: https://www.facebook.com/azurepixels
Wongtwothree Photography: https://www.facebook.com/WongtwothreePhotography
YassiR KetchuM Photography: https://www.facebook.com/YassirKetchuMPhotography

North Carolina
ConQuest Images: https://www.facebook.com/ConQuestImages
Fang Fox Photography: https://www.facebook.com/FangFoxPhotos
Jubai Strube: https://www.facebook.com/CosplayHeroes1991
Midday Enchantments Photography: https://www.facebook.com/middayenchantments-photography
N3 Photography: https://www.facebook.com/N3Photography
Ripptowne Photography: https://www.facebook.com/RipptownePhotography

Ohio
Doug Sanders Photography: https://www.facebook.com/pages/Doug-Sanders-Photography/206198366109311
Cerulean Photography: https://www.facebook.com/pages/Cerulean-Photography/242949702432475
Kayneth Fotografisch Werke: https://www.facebook.com/KaynethFotografischWerke
K. M. Keller Films: https://www.facebook.com/K.M.KellerFilms
KRN Photography: https://www.facebook.com/pages/KRN-Photography/136248633243789
Krunchy Studios: https://www.facebook.com/KrunchyStudios
The Portrait Dude (cosplay photography): https://www.facebook.com/theportraitdudecosplay

Oklahoma
Sokol Photography: https://www.facebook.com/pages/Sokol-Photography/126881030657318

Pennsylvania
Adorkable Photography: https://www.facebook.com/adorkablephotography
Heartshine Photography: http://heartshinephotography.weebly.com/
Rebekah Shultz Photography: https://www.facebook.com/RebekahShultzPhotography
Shecktor Photography: https://www.facebook.com/ShecktorPhotography
Tommyish Cosplay and Photography: https://www.facebook.com/Tommyishh

South Carolina
City Light Studio: Sector C: https://www.facebook.com/CityLightCosplay
CoryD Photography: https://www.facebook.com/CoryDPhotography
Double Stomp Productions: https://www.facebook.com/DoubleStompProductions
James Pittman Gallery (.jpg): https://www.facebook.com/jamespittmangallery
JM Photography and Design: https://www.facebook.com/jessicalmphotography
Starrfall Photography: https://www.facebook.com/starrfallphotography

Tennessee
Chris Auditore Photography (Tullahoma): https://www.facebook.com/Chrisauditorephotography/
Iconiq Cosplay Photography: https://www.facebook.com/Iconiqcosplay
One Time Hero Photography: https://www.facebook.com/OneTimeHeroPhotography

Texas
Aaron Stone, Fearless Ace Photography: https://www.facebook.com/FearlessPortraits
Fearless Portraits: https://www.facebook.com/fearlessace
MEChan Cosplay Photography: https://www.facebook.com/mechancosplayphotography
NJD Photography: https://www.facebook.com/PhotosxNJD

Virginia and Washington, D.C.
Amit Muntasir Photography: https://www.facebook.com/AmitMMphotography
Blue Shell Photography: https://www.facebook.com/Blue.Shell.Photos
Crunchy Spart Photography: https://www.facebook.com/CrunchySpartPhotography
Dancing Squirrel Photography: https://www.facebook.com/DancingSquirrelPhotography
Darkfox Photography: https://www.facebook.com/DarkfoxPhotography
Howell's Visions Photography: https://www.facebook.com/HowellsVisionsPhotography
Kennmax Photography: http://www.kennmax.com
Kenshin Photography: https://www.facebook.com/KenshinPhotography
Kreation Studios: https://www.facebook.com/kreationstu
Lee Love Photography: http://www.leelove.com
Munchkin Photography: https://www.facebook.com/MunchkinPhotosbyHeather
Top Secret Press: http://tinyurl.com/osz9yak

Washington
Bill Hinsee Photography: https://www.facebook.com/home.php

Canada

Ontario
A Lanna Mode: https://www.facebook.com/AlannaMode
Crosswing Photography and Productions: https://www.facebook.com/CrosswingPhotographyProductions
Don Dolce Photography: https://www.facebook.com/DonDolcePhotography
Etoile Star Photography: https://www.facebook.com/EtoileStarPhotography
Krystal Clear Photography: https://www.facebook.com/KrystalClearPhoto
Zealous Photography: https://www.facebook.com/ZealousPhotographer

Saskatchewan
    Randee Gee Photographee: https://www.facebook.com/RandyGeePhotographee

International

United Kingdom
    Superhero Creations by Adam Jay: https://www.facebook.com/superherocreations

NOTE

1. Philip Ng, "Cosplay Photographers," Philip Ng Facebook status, accessed April 28, 2015, http://goo.gl/C1IVhQ.

Appendix E

Cosplay Websites and Blogs Directory

Note: This list is heavily based on a fantastic resource put together by Christopher Wanamaker, which is a list of places to submit cosplay photos for publication or posting to the sites.[1] Wanamaker updates it monthly. It is available as a file in the Promote Your Cosplay Page Facebook group (http://tinyurl.com/olalp54).

- All Cosplayers Are Equal: https://www.facebook.com/ACE.SATX
- Best Black Cosplay: http://tinyurl.com/kbfnuoj
- Best Cosplays: http://tinyurl.com/o2kzf7o
- Comics Alliance: http://tinyurl.com/p46ylmv
- Cosfluff (plus-size cosplay): https://www.facebook.com/Cosfluff101
- Cosplay: https://www.facebook.com/therealcosplay
- Cosplay: https://www.facebook.com/cosplaayy
- Cosplay +Sz: https://www.facebook.com/pages/Cosplay-Sz/686413854735774
- Cosplay.com: http://www.cosplay.com
- Cosplay Advice: http://cosplayadvice.tumblr.com
- Cosplay Corner: http://tinyurl.com/kapvdvc
- Cosplay Craze: https://www.facebook.com/cosplaycraze
- Cosplay Equalist: http://tinyurl.com/ka4vk6j
- Cosplay for All: http://cosplayforall.tumblr.com
- Cosplay Fever: https://www.facebook.com/cosplayfever
- Cosplay in America: http://cosplayinamerica.tumblr.com
- Cosplay on Pinterest: https://www.pinterest.com/explore/cosplay
- Cosplayers: https://www.facebook.com/officialcosplayers
- Cosplaying while Latino: https://www.facebook.com/CosplayingWhileLatino
- Cosplays and Cosplayers: https://www.facebook.com/cosplaysycosplayers
- Cosplay Worldwide: https://www.facebook.com/Amateurcosplaying
- Costuming.org: http://costuming.org
- Creative Cosplay: https://www.facebook.com/CreativeCosplayCommunity
- DC Comics Cosplay: https://www.facebook.com/dccosplay
- Geeks Are Sexy: http://www.geeksaresexy.net

- Hot & Geeky: https://www.facebook.com/hotngeeky
- I Love Cosplay: https://www.facebook.com/lovingcosplay
- Majestic Cosplay: https://www.facebook.com/majesticcosplay
- Marvel Comics Cosplay: https://www.facebook.com/marvelcosplay
- Men vs Cosplay: https://www.facebook.com/menvscosplay
- Men vs Cosplay EU: https://www.facebook.com/menvscosplayeu
- Nothing but Cosplay: https://www.facebook.com/nothingbutcosplay
- Over 30 Cosplay: https://www.facebook.com/pages/Over-30-Cosplay/14116171909131524
- Pepakura Library: https://www.facebook.com/groups/PepakuraLibrary/
- Plus!Size Cosplay: https://www.facebook.com/plussizedcosplay
- Plus Size Cosplay: https://www.facebook.com/PlusSizeCosplayAppreciation
- Popculture Uncovered: http://popcultureuncovered.com/category/cosplay-life/
- Sexy Cosplay Girls: http://tinyurl.com/oo9y875
- Southern Cospatality: https://www.facebook.com/SouthernCospitality
- Super Cosplay Girls: https://www.facebook.com/SCGcosplay
- Super Cosplay Guys: https://www.facebook.com/SCGuyscosplay
- Super Hero Costuming Forum: http://thesuperherocostumingforum.tumblr.com
- The Art of Cosplay Page: https://www.facebook.com/ARTCOSPLAYPAGE
- The Replica Prop Forum: http://www.therpf.com
- United Prop Builders Prop Tutorials: http://tinyurl.com/lfhkt9v
- We Are Cosplayers: https://www.facebook.com/wearecostplayers
- Women of Comic Book Cosplay: https://www.facebook.com/comicbookcosplay
- Women of Crossplay: http://women-of-crossplay.tumblr.com
- Woman vs Cosplay: https://www.facebook.com/womenvscosplay

Magazines

- *4Cosplay Magazine*: https://www.facebook.com/4CosplayMagazine
- *CAA Photoshoot Magazine*: http://caa.w.pw/magazine/
- *Cosplay Culture* magazine: http://cosplayculturemagazine.com/print-magazine
- *Cos Culture Magazine*: https://www.facebook.com/cosculturemagazine
- *Cosplayers Among Us*: https://facebook.com/cosplayersamongus
- *Cosplay Famous*: http://cosplayfamous.com
- *Cosplay Fanatic*: https://www.facebook.com/pages/Cosplay-Fanatic/622939641109458
- *Cosplay Gen*: http://www.cosplaygen.com
- *Cosplay Weekly*: http://www.cosplayweekly.com
- *Generate: A Cosplay Magazine*: https://www.facebook.com/GenerateACM
- *iCosplay* magazine: http://www.icosplaymag.com
- *La Vida en Cosplay*: http://www.lavidaencosplay.com
- *My Cosplay Girl*: http://mycosplaygirl.com
- *Nerd Caliber*: http://nerdcaliber.com
- *We Rise Mag*: http://www.werisemag.com
- *Word of the Nerd*: http://www.wordofthenerdonline.com

NOTE

1. Christopher Wanamaker, "Cosplay list.docx, Version 1," Promote Your Cosplay Page Facebook group, accessed April 23, 2015, https://www.facebook.com/groups/446542822158899/666051683541344.

Resources

Must-Have Cosplay Resources

BOOKS

Alinger, B. Star Wars *Costumes: The Original Trilogy*. San Francisco, CA: Chronicle Books, 2014.

Ashcraft, B., and L. Plunkett. *Cosplay World*. Munich: Prestel, 2014.

Beatty, S., and D. Wallace. *The DC Comics Encyclopedia: The Definitive Guide to the Characters of the DC Universe*. New York: DK Pub, 2008.

Clements, J., and H. McCarthy. *The Anime Encyclopedia, 3rd Revised Edition: A Century of Japanese Animation*. New York: Stone Bridge Press, 2015.

Cowsill, A., A. Irvine, M. K. Manning, M. McAvennie, D. Wallace, and L. Gilbert. *DC Comics: A Visual History*. New York: DK Publishing, 2014.

DeFalco, T., and A. Dougall. *Marvel Encyclopedia: The Definitive Guide to the Characters of the Marvel Universe*. New York: DK Publishing, 2014.

Doran, Bill. *Foam Armorsmithing*. Vol. 1, *Design, Templating, & Fabrication*. Punished Props.

———. *Foam Armorsmithing*. Vol. 2, *Finishing & Painting*. Punished Props.

———. *Foam Armorsmithing*. Vol. 3, *Undersuits, Straps, & Lights*. Punished Props.

García, H. *A Geek in Japan: Discovering the Land of Manga, Anime, Zen, and the Tea Ceremony*. Tokyo: Tuttle Pub, 2010.

Gleason, K., K. W. Jeter, and D. M. Pho. *Anatomy of Steampunk: The Fashion of Victorian Futurism*. New York: Race Point Publishing, 2013.

Han, Y., A. Deblasio, and J. Marsocci. *1,000 Incredible Costume & Cosplay Ideas: A Showcase of Creative Characters in Anime, Manga, Video Games, Movies, Comics, and More!* Minneapolis: Minneapolis Rockport Publishers, 2013.

Loborik, J., A. Gibson, and M. Laing. Doctor Who*: Character Encyclopedia*. London: DK Pub, 2013.

Quindt, Svetlana. *Armor Pattern Collection: Female Version*. Nuremberg, Germany: Author, 2014.

———. *Armor Pattern Collection: Male Version*. Nuremberg, Germany: Author, 2014.

———. *The Book of Cosplay Armor Making: With Worbla and Wonderflex*. Nuremberg, Germany: Author, 2014.

———. *The Book of Cosplay Lights: Getting Started with LEDs*. Nuremberg, Germany: Author, 2014.

———. *The Book of Cosplay Painting: With Brushes and Acrylics*. Nuremberg, Germany: Author, 2014.

———. *The Book of Prop Making: With Foam and Worbla*. Nuremberg, Germany: Author, 2014.

Reeder, D. *Papier-Mâché Monsters: Turn Trinkets and Trash into Magnificent Monstrosities*. Layton, UT: Gibbs Smith, 2009.

Richards, J. Doctor Who *50: The Essential Guide*. London: London BBC Children's Books, 2013.

Ruditis, P. Star Trek, *the Visual Dictionary: The Ultimate Guide to Characters, Aliens, and Technology*. London: DK, 2013.

Snider, B. T. *DC Comics: The Ultimate Character Guide*. New York: DK Pub, 2011.

Star Wars *Year by Year: A Visual Chronicle*. London: DK Pub, 2010.

Thomas, R., and J. Baker. *75 Years of Marvel: From the Golden Age to the Silver Screen*. Cologne: Taschen, 2014.

ARTICLES AND THESES

Hale, Matthew. "Cosplay: Intertextuality, Public Texts, and the Body Fantastic." *Western Folklore* 73, no.1 (Winter 2014).

Leng, Rachel Hui Ying. "Gender, Sexuality, and Cosplay: A Case Study of Male-to-Female Crossplay." *The Phoenix Papers: First Edition*, April 2013, 89–110. http://nrs.harvard.edu/urn-3:HUL.InstRepos: 13481274.

Lotecki, Ashley. "Cosplay Culture: The Development of Interactive and Living Art through Play." Master's thesis, Ryerson University, 2012.

Rosenberg, Robin S., and Andrea M. Letamendi. "Expressions of Fandom: Findings from a Psychological Survey of Cosplay and Costume Wear." *Intensities: The Journal of Cult Media* 5 (Spring/Summer 2013). http://intensitiescultmedia.com.

Taylor, Jayme Rebecca. "Convention Cosplay: Subversive Potential in Anime Fandom." Master's thesis, The University of British Columbia, 2009, 5–23.

PRESENTATIONS

Aarant, Megan, and Natalie Couch. "Got Fandom? How Mini-Cons Can Transform Libraries and Communities." Presented as part of the Georgia Library webinar series, February 25, 2015. http://tinyurl .com/o8oy8qj.

Mairn, Chad. "Organizing a Successful Comic Con at Your Library." Presented on October 1, 2014. http://tinyurl.com/pwe8p6w.

Index

About the Author

Ellyssa Kroski is the director of information technology at the New York Law Institute, as well as an award-winning editor and author of thirty-four books, including *Law Librarianship in the Digital Age*, for which she won the AALL's 2014 Joseph L. Andrews Legal Literature Award. Her ten-book technology series, The Tech Set, won the ALA's Best Book in Library Literature Award in 2011. She is a librarian, an adjunct faculty member at the Pratt Institute, and an international conference speaker. She blogs at *Cosplay, Comics, and Geek Culture in Libraries*. Her professional portfolio is located at http://www.ellyssakroski.com.

Ellyssa is also an avid cosplayer and has appeared on TLC's *Cake Boss* TV show, as well as in the official music video for New York Comic Con and many other events. Her cosplay portfolio can be found at http://giallogirl.com. Contact her at ellyssakroski@yahoo.com.

ELLYSSA ON SOCIAL MEDIA

Twitter: https://twitter.com/ellyssa
LinkedIn: https://www.linkedin.com/in/ellyssa
Professional Facebook: https://www.facebook.com/ellyssa
Cosplay Facebook page: https://www.facebook.com/giallogirl